Church Women

Probing History with Girls

Nurturing the
Spirituality of Girls

Church Women

Probing History with Girls

Laurie Delgatto

with Marilyn Kielbasa

Voices;
Nurturing the
Spirituality of Girls

Saint Mary's Press
Christian Brothers Publications
Winona, Minnesota

The following authors contributed to this manual:
- Sheila Bourelly, Chicago, Illinois
- Alice Davis, Shorewood, Wisconsin
- Kat Hodapp, Louisville, Kentucky
- Julia Keller, Pebble Beach, California
- Pamela Reidy, Worcester, Massachusetts

A special thank-you to the following girls from Orlando, Florida; Birmingham, Alabama; Lackawanna, New York; Boston, Massachusetts; and Winona, Minnesota, for contributing their thoughts about what they would like the world to know about them. Their quotes are used in the prayer "These Stones Will Shout."
- Alicia, Anna, Ashley, Cara, Emily, Frances, Jaclyn, Jessica, Jessica, Jessica, Julie, Liza, Lizbeth, Megan, and Stefanie

 Genuine recycled paper with 10% post-consumer waste. Printed with soy-based ink.

The publishing team included Cheryl Drivdahl, copy editor; Lynn Riska, production editor and typesetter; Cindi Ramm, design director; Cären Yang, cover designer; back cover images copyright © Rubberball Productions; manufactured by the production services department of Saint Mary's Press.

Ann Coron, cover artist, Winona Voices Group, Winona, MN

The acknowledgments continue on page 136.

Printed in the United States of America

Printing: 9 8 7 6 5 4 3 2 1

Year: 2010 09 08 07 06 05 04 03 02

ISBN 0-88489-701-X

Library of Congress Cataloging-in-Publication Data

Delgatto, Laurie.
    Church women : probing history with girls / Laurie Delgatto, with Marilyn Kielbasa.
        p. cm. — (Voices)
ISBN 0-88489-701-X (pbk.)
        1. Church group work with teenage girls. 2. Catholic women—Biography—Study and teaching.
3. Teenage girls—Religious life. I. Kielbasa, Marilyn. II. Title. III. Voices (Winona, Minn.)
BX2347.8.Y7 D45 2002
282'.092'2—dc21
                                                                                              2001006634

To my grandmother Gertrude Reilly, whose life can be defined only as phenomenal.
And for my sisters, Lisa and Melissa, who carry on the tradition.

—Laurie Delgatto

We thank the following people, who helped to shape the final chapter of this book. Each generously and vulnerably shared his or her story about an extraordinary young woman: Carrie Mach.

Richard Bancke

Kristen Considine

Fr. Gerald Feierfeil

Phyllis Harrington

Fr. David Hogan

Sue Hrasky

Lisa Niedergeses

Linda Shoemaker

Gina Shook

We also express deep gratitude to Carrie's parents, Rick and Ann Mach, and to her friends, who loved and knew her so well. And most especially, we acknowledge Carrie herself. We will always remember how she gave others the courage to give.

—Laurie Delgatto and Marilyn Kielbasa

Contents

Part B: Phenomenal Female Visionaries and Prophets

Introduction

"You are made in the image of God." That simple statement is the heart of spirituality—a profound statement about who we are and who we are becoming. There is no more important mantra for adults to communicate as they parent, teach, minister, and pray with young people.

The journey to adulthood has always been a time of transition. Those who walk with adolescents know that the journey is also unique for each person. In fact, recent studies confirm the age-old intuitive sense that girls and boys experience life in ways that are unique to their gender. If gender differences affect physical, emotional, and psychological development, then certainly, spirituality is shaped as well by feminine or masculine perspectives.

For girls in this country at the turn of the millennium, opportunities for equality are greater than for girls in any previous generation. Still, psychologists, educators, ministers, and parents know that the risks and issues that confront young females seem rooted in a different reality than those that face young males. Brought up in the crucible of a media world, girls continue to receive messages that beauty and body are more important than mind and spirit. Told that they can do anything, they too often engage in behaviors that endanger them more than empower them. In the interest of "being nice," they abdicate their voice to males, exhibiting a dramatic drop in self-esteem in their adolescent years.

Girls experience life in terms of relationships. While their male counterparts charge headlong into separation and independence, young women, by nature and nurture, seem predisposed to connectedness and intimacy. Psychologists like Carol Gilligan *(In a Different Voice)* and Mary Pipher *(Reviving Ophelia)* have brought attention to the life of girls, spawning an entire genre of literature aimed at addressing the phenomenon of the female adolescent experience. Addressing young women's psychosocial world is a good beginning, but few experts in the field of girls' development have ventured into the realm of spirituality.

Spirituality is about relationship—relationship with the One who created us. It is about loving and living out a call to become the kind of person God created us to be. Girls need to hear this message, embrace it, and live it. They need guidance to challenge a culture that contradicts their sacredness; they need adults who will listen to them, relate with them, and walk with them, reminding them of their destiny, reminding them, "You are made in the image of God."

"Herstory" of the Voices Project

The Voices Project is the realization of the dream of a national team of female educators, youth ministers, parents, and mentors who have a special concern for the spirituality of girls. They envisioned a multifaceted initiative that would bring together the energy of the girls' movement and the wisdom of women's spirituality. Their dream was a convergence of the work of psychologists Mary Pipher and Carol Gilligan with the work of Catholic writers like Maria Harris and Elizabeth Johnson. As a result of listening sessions with girls from around the country, the team identified the need for resources for adults who work with girls in Catholic school and parish settings. One response to that need is the Voices series.

Overview of the Voices Series

The Voices series consists of six manuals that present strategies to use with adolescent girls in schools, parishes, and single-gender settings. The authors and consultants of the series have extensive experience working with girls in both coed and single-gender situations. The manuals they have produced are different from one another in content and focus, yet all share the same purpose: to help girls embrace the true meaning of the phrase "created in the image of God," a profound statement about who they are and who they are becoming. This manual, *Church Women: Probing History with Girls,* is one of the results; the other manuals in the series are as follows:

- *Awakening: Challenging the Culture with Girls* offers a variety of activities to help girls critique the culture for both its negative and its positive influences.
- *Retreats: Deepening the Spirituality of Girls* presents seven retreats on themes such as friendship, media, and childhood myths. Also included is a retreat for mothers and daughters.
- *Prayer: Celebrating and Reflecting with Girls* provides ideas for community prayer services and suggestions for enriching girls' personal prayer life.
- *Biblical Women: Exploring Their Stories with Girls* suggests ways to help girls get to know the women in the Scriptures and examine the roles they played in communities of faith and the beginnings of the church.
- *Seeking: Doing Theology with Girls* offers methods for exploring and discussing theological and moral issues from the perspective of women.

Where and When to Use the Voices Series

The Voices resource manuals can be used in a variety of settings, though they are intended for use with girls in single-gender groups. The rationale for meeting in single-gender settings is particularly compelling for young women. Numerous studies indicate that girls are much more likely to speak up, express their opinion, and be genuinely heard in "just girl" groups. Some topics related to growing up and finding one's way in society are difficult for females to discuss in the presence of males. Imparting the particular wisdom of women to girls, and of men to boys, is a time-honored practice that can be highly effective when used occasionally in educational, church, and social institutions.

Unless you are on the staff of an all-girls high school, finding opportunities for single-gender gatherings can be a challenge; consider these suggestions:

- Offer gender-specific electives within a school or parish catechetical setting.
- Work with Scout groups, which are already gender specific.
- Form "just girl" groups that meet beyond the typical school day or parish youth night.
- Establish weekly or monthly sessions within the school or parish schedule, at which girls and boys discuss related topics separately. Subsequent discussion with both groups together can lead to greater understanding between the sexes.
- Create mother-daughter or mentor-mentee discussion groups.
- Organize diocesan days for "just girls" or "just boys," or both.
- Arrange retreats and youth rallies that have gender-specific components or work-shops.

Who Might Use the Voices Series

The six resource manuals in the Voices series may be used by coordinators of youth ministry, directors of religious education, teachers in Catholic schools, campus ministers, youth ministers in parish settings, Girl Scout and Camp Fire leaders, parents, mentors, and other adults who work with girls ages ten through nineteen. Flexible enough for single-sex groups in any setting, the manuals' ideas are designed to engage girls in both headwork and heart work, challenging them to think while nurturing their spirit.

Overview of This Manual

The strategies in *Church Women: Probing History with Girls* are designed to help girls discover the richness of women's contributions to the life of the church throughout its history. Part A of the manual focuses on saints and mystics. Part B develops the theme of visionaries and prophets and focuses on women who have made recent contributions and have influenced the church in the modern world.

We could have included hundreds of women in this manual, for women have been impacting the life of the church from its very beginning. However, we had to make some choices. The women in this manual were selected with certain criteria in mind:

- They are not represented in the Scriptures. Women whose stories are known through the Scriptures are presented in another manual in the Voices series, *Biblical Women: Exploring Their Stories with Girls*.
- Their stories are generally not well known to girls. For example, we did not include Mother Teresa because most girls have heard her story since they were young, in classes, in homilies, and in books.

- Their stories expand the stereotypical view of feminine sanctity that has been promulgated through the ages. Far from being passive, submissive, and yielding, these women challenged their world and our own.
- Their work is likely to enliven the hearts of young people and ignite their passion for justice, inspiring girls to emulate the women's spiritual life and to continue their work.

How to Use This Manual

You may present the material in this manual in its entirety, or you may select pieces to supplement your regular curriculum in a school or religious education program. Many of the activities have connections to liturgical seasons or church observances. For example, you might use the material on Sr. Helen Prejean during Lent, the rosary activity "Prayer: A Decade with Dorothy Day" in October, or an activity on Sr. Thea Bowman during Black Catholic History Month. All the chapters are formatted as follows:

Thematic Activities

Each chapter contains several fully developed activities, most of which are designed for a time frame of 30 to 60 minutes. The first activity in each chapter is biographical and therefore should be used before any other activity in that chapter. Other thematic activities develop ideas, charisms, the devotion, or the zeal of the woman and her work. Many of the thematic activities offer one or more variations, or different approaches for presenting the material.

Options and Actions

Most of the chapters include additional activities to support the learning process. These provide good follow-up for the thematic activities and allow for age-appropriate assimilation of the material. They might include multigenerational interaction, service options, and social action.

Resource Materials

Some of the chapters provide a list of resources—such as print, video, and Internet—for more exploration. In addition, some activities mention resources that address the person or themes covered. Materials published by Saint Mary's Press may be ordered from the press's Web site, *www.smp.org,* or by calling 800-533-8095.

Background Information

Most of the chapters include background information on the woman and her work. This material is given to help you guide the girls in their discussion and exploration of the topic.

Notes

Space is provided for you to jot down ideas, reminders, and additional resources as you use the chapter materials.

Handouts and Resources

All the necessary handouts and resources for a chapter are found at the end of the chapter.

How to Get Started

Know the Material

Read each chapter or activity before you facilitate it, and use it creatively to meet the needs of your particular group of girls. In particular, look for ways to make the material most accessible for the girls' ages and for the size of the group. All the suggestions in this manual can be used with girls ages fourteen to nineteen. Some material is also appropriate for younger girls. Most of the activities in this manual are designed for groups of twenty to thirty young people, but can easily be adapted for any size group.

Know the Young People

When you have a wide variety of ages together, keep in mind the following differences between young adolescents and older teens:

- Young adolescents think in concrete terms and may not yet be capable of considering some topics abstractly.
- Young adolescents generally need more physical movement than older teens do. You can address that need through simple activities such as forming small groups for discussion and moving to different halves of the room to indicate the answer to a yes-or-no question.
- When they are working in small groups, young adolescents do better with an adult or older teen leading them. Groups of older teens can often be left alone for discussions.
- Older teens can usually handle open-ended assignments, but young adolescents respond better to writing exercises and discussions if they are led. For example, a junior in high school can be expected to write a letter to God about a certain topic on a blank sheet of notebook paper, whereas a sixth grader will be more focused with sentence-starters to guide different parts of the letter.

Create a Welcoming Environment

When possible, adapt the physical space to allow for open discussion and sharing. Consider moving chairs into a circle or inviting everyone to sit on the floor, at times. Groups that meet regularly may want to create a sacred space for ritual, using candles, fabric, music, favorite statues, sculptures, and images. Encourage the girls to be involved in creating that space and keeping it special.

Create a Safe Environment

When involving mothers, mentors, and other adults, provide written guidelines and even training in group leadership to help them understand the process and dynamics of the group. Consider the following guidelines for any adults who work with the group:

- To hear girls at the level necessary for meaningful interaction, adults need first to listen to themselves and to remember their own adolescence (Patricia H. Davis, *Beyond Nice,* p. 119).
- Girls need adults who will listen to them and affirm them even when their questions and actions seem uncomfortably challenging, and adults who will allow themselves to be questioned at deep levels (p. 120).
- Girls need confidentiality in any group that engages them in deep thinking, feeling, and sharing. Yet, they and the adults who lead them also need to know when to go beyond the resources of the group to seek help.
- Girls need adults who will help them be countercultural in ways that bring animation and love to their life, their community, and their world (p. 121).
- To help girls recognize and nurture their own relationship with God, communities of faith need to listen to and learn from them and take them seriously, with engaged hearts, minds, and souls (p. 121).

General Resources

Print

Cowan, Tom. *The Way of the Saints: Prayers, Practices, and Meditations.* New York: Perigee Books, 2000. This book contains more than two hundred biographies of saints, a history of sainthood, and an explanation of the canonization process. Readers will also find prayers, practices, and meditations inspired by each saint.

Jones, Kathleen. *Women Saints: Lives of Faith and Courage.* Maryknoll, NY: Orbis Books, 1999. This book highlights forty women of chronological, geographical, and spiritual variety, expanding the traditional view of feminine sanctity and challenging readers to lead a more authentic Christian life.

Madigan, Shawn, ed. *Mystics, Visionaries, and Prophets: A Historical Anthology of Women's Spiritual Writings.* Minneapolis: Fortress Press, 1998. This compilation presents the writings of twenty-seven women representing seventeen centuries of church history. It also includes informative historical introductions and bibliographies.

Morgan, Robert. *On This Day: 365 Amazing and Inspiring Stories About Saints, Martyrs, and Heroes.* Nashville, TN: Nelson Reference, 1997. This year's worth of stories about mystics, reformers, missionary heroes, and modern-day saints and prophets gives readers glimpses into church history.

Internet

www.americancatholic.org. St. Anthony Messenger Press.

www.catholic.org. Catholic Online. This site contains a large collection of facts and information concerning saints and angels. Its Saints Index is an exhaustive list of information pertaining to the various saints.

www.catholic-forum.com/saints/indexsnt.htm. Catholic Community Forum. This site offers information about and profiles of patron saints, including portraits, biographical information, areas of patronage, prayers, links to related sites, and readings.

www.disciplesnow.com. Disciples Now. This Web-based ministry and informational resource for youth focuses on the traditions, life, and mission of the Catholic church.

www.nwhp.org. National Women's History Project. This Web site and its sponsoring organization are dedicated to recognizing the accomplishments of women by providing information and educational material and programs.

Voices Internet Resources

Log on to the Voices Web site, *www.smp.org/voices,* for ideas, activities, resources, and links. This Web site is updated weekly.

Your Comments or Suggestions

Saint Mary's Press wants to know your reactions to the strategies in the Voices series. We are also interested in new strategies for use with adolescent girls. If you have a comment or suggestion, please write c/o Voices, Saint Mary's Press, 702 Terrace Heights, Winona, MN 55987-1320; use the "Contact Us" page at *www.smp.org/voices;* or contact the editorial development department through our toll-free number, 800-533-8095. Your ideas will help improve future editions of these manuals.

Part A

Phenomenal Female Saints and Mystics

Julian of Norwich

Overview

There are many lessons for adolescent girls in the life and writings of Julian of Norwich. Her love of creation, use of imagination, images of God, and belief that all will be well can lead the girls in your group to deepen their own spirituality and grow in their faith.

This chapter contains activities to help the young women explore three major themes expressed in Julian's writings. The activities are appropriate for girls in junior high and high school, though some adaptations may be needed, depending on your situation.

Thematic Activities

Who Was Julian of Norwich? (5 minutes)

Preparation

○ Prepare to give the girls the background information on the life, spirituality, and writings of Julian of Norwich from the end of this chapter. Become familiar enough with the information that you can share it in a storytelling style. The material is taken from *Praying with Julian of Norwich,* by Gloria Durka (Winona, MN: Saint Mary's Press, 1989). It might be helpful for you to have a copy of that book for your own reference and enrichment.

Begin the exploration of Julian by offering a brief biography in your own words. Then, as you lead each activity, share relevant information from the section on Julian's spirituality.

Images of the Trinity (45–55 minutes)

Preparation

○ Read step 2, decide which method of creating stained glass windows you will use, and gather the appropriate supplies.

1. Julian's words. Explain that one of Julian's outstanding traits as a theologian was her imagination. For example, she spoke of the Trinity in terms of maker, protector, and lover. Read aloud the following passage from Julian's *Showings:*

◉ "Suddenly the Trinity filled my heart full of the greatest joy, and I understood that it will be so in heaven without end to all who will come there. For the Trinity is God, God is the Trinity. The Trinity is our maker, the Trinity is our protector, the Trinity is our everlasting lover, the Trinity is our endless joy and our bliss" (p. 181).

2. Divide the girls into three groups and assign each group a different one of the images maker, protector, and lover. Announce that each group will create a stained glass window that captures what its image is all about. Tell the groups each to spend some time brainstorming possibilities and then create their window.

Propose one of the following methods for creating the windows. The second method is likely to take longer than the first.
- *Method 1.* Use markers or crayons to create shapes and colors in the style of stained glass on a sheet of white poster board.
- *Method 2.* Cut the outline of the window from a sheet of black poster board. Cut pieces of "glass" from tissue paper in various colors, and then glue or tape the pieces to the back of the poster board outline.

3. When the groups have completed their windows, invite them to present their work to everyone and to explain it. Post the windows where they can be seen and appreciated by the parish or school community.

4. Lead a discussion using questions like the ones that follow:
◉ How are Julian's images of maker, protector, and lover different from the traditional images of Father, Son, and Holy Spirit? How are they similar?
◉ What other images show the relationship between the Triune God and humanity?

Variation. Create a list of images for the Trinity that emerge from the discussion. Use the various images in future gatherings whenever you call the girls to prayer.

The Worth and Beauty of Creation

1. Julian's words. Explain that during a time when the world was not appreciated for itself, Julian saw the worth and beauty in all of God's creation, great and small. Read aloud the following text from Julian's *Showings:*

⊚ "[God] showed me something small, no bigger than a hazelnut, lying in the palm of my hand, as it seemed to me, and it was as round as a ball. I looked at it with the eye of my understanding and thought: What can this be? . . .

"In this little thing I saw three properties. The first is that God made it, the second is that God loves it, the third is that God preserves it. But what did I see in it? It is that God is the Creator and the protector and the lover" (p. 183).

2. Lead one or more of the following exercises.

Symbol Sharing (10–20 minutes)

Preparation
○ Set up a prayer table in the center of your meeting space.
○ Ask the girls to bring in small items that remind them of God's creation, God's love, and God's protection.

Gather the girls in a circle, with the prayer table at the center. Invite each girl to share with the group the items she brought to represent the three properties about which Julian wrote. As each girl finishes, invite her to add the items to the prayer table, speaking these ideas from Julian's passage as she does so: "God made it. God loves it. God protects and preserves it."

Variation 1. Do this exercise in a park or another natural setting. Instead of asking the girls to bring items from home, send them on a quiet walk to find three items that remind them of God's creation, God's love, and God's protection.

Variation 2. Combine this exercise with the next exercise, "Message in Movement," and suggest that the girls include their symbolic items in their movement prayer.

Message in Movement (30–45 minutes)

Preparation
○ You may want to provide a variety of music for the girls to choose from.

Create small groups of six to eight girls. Announce that each group is to develop a short dance, mime, or motion sketch that expresses the three properties noted in Julian's message "God made it. God loves it. God preserves and protects it."

Invite each group to present its creation to everyone, preferably within the context of prayer.

A Twist on the Creation Story (10–20 minutes)

Read one or both of the Creation stories from the first and second chapters of the Book of Genesis. Lead a discussion focused around questions like these:

⊚ How does the passage from Julian's writing compare with the story (or stories) from Genesis?

⊚ What might Julian have changed in the Creation story (or stories) if she had written it (or them)?

Conclude by reading (or rereading) the first Creation story from Genesis. Instead of repeating, "And God saw that it was good," at the end of each day of Creation, call the girls to respond: "God made it. God loves it. God preserves and protects it."

All Shall Be Well

1. Julian's words. Explain that one central message from Julian of Norwich is a simple message of optimism—that all shall be well. It is an important message for each of us to take to heart. It is a statement of faith and trust in God. Read aloud the following text from Julian's *Showings:*

⊚ "And so our good Lord answered to all the questions and doubts which I could raise, saying most comfortingly: I may make all things well, and I can make all things well, and I shall make all things well, and I will make all things well; and you will see yourself that every kind of thing will be well" (p. 229).

2. Lead one or more of the following exercises.

Bookmark Reminders (15–30 minutes)

Provide a variety of art supplies and stiff papers. Encourage the girls to create bookmarks for themselves, friends, and family members, with the phrase "All shall be well" on them. The bookmarks can be embellished with tassels, glitter, and so forth.

Variation. Use this exercise as a fund-raiser for your group. Have the girls create and decorate a wide variety of bookmarks with the phrase "All shall be well" on them, and sell them at a parish or school function.

Music Search (10–40 minutes)

Invite the girls to bring in popular music with lyrics that have a message similar to Julian's assurance that all shall be well. Invite the girls to play the songs for the group and to explain why they chose the pieces. Discuss the lyrics of each song with the group using questions like the ones that follow:

⊚ How is the message of the song the same as Julian's message? How are the two messages different?

⊚ According to the song, what will make all things well?

⊚ How does life look when all things are well?

Scripture Search (15–20 minutes)

Encourage the girls to find Scripture passages that express comfort in the same way that "All shall be well" does. Use those passages as the basis for a journal-writing exercise or art projects. Some passages that may be used are as follows:

- Ps. 23:1–6 (The Lord is my shepherd.)
- Isa. 43:1–5 (Be not afraid.)
- Isa. 49:13–16 (We are inscribed on God's hand.)
- Matt. 11:28–30 (Come to me; I will give you rest.)
- Rev. 21:5–7 (I make all things new.)

Reflection Questions (15–20 minutes)

If the girls know one another well and are willing to share their thoughts, lead a discussion or a sharing partners exercise, using questions like the ones that follow. You can also use questions like these for reflection, journal writing, or prayer time.

- ◉ Are you an optimist or a pessimist? Give an example that demonstrates your preferred style.
- ◉ What does Julian's message "All shall be well" mean to you?
- ◉ When have you felt that all was well? When have you felt the opposite? How did you feel God's presence or absence in each situation?
- ◉ Where in your life right now do you need to hear and believe Julian's message that all shall be well?
- ◉ Who else do you know who needs to hear and believe that message?

Variation. Begin the study of Julian's optimism by leading the girls through a personal style inventory that helps them understand if they are an optimist or a pessimist. Such an inventory can be found on pages 46–48 of *Finding Your Personal Style,* by Marilyn Kielbasa, in the Horizons Program (Winona, MN: Saint Mary's Press, 1996).

Options and Actions

- As part of a prayer, suggest that the girls use Julian's message as a mantra that emphasizes God's love and care for each of us: "God made me. God loves me. God protects me."
- With the girls, create posters, PowerPoint slides, T-shirts, murals, or other eye-catching devices on which you present key phrases or main themes of Julian's spirituality, such as "God made it. God loves it. God preserves and protects it" and "All shall be well." Place the devices in strategic locations while you are discussing each particular aspect of Julian.
- Create journal or reflection pages, with a quote from Julian at the top of each one. Distribute the pages and invite the girls to spend quiet time writing about a word or phrase that strikes them in each quote. You could also provide reflection questions, Scripture passages, or other guidelines for writing.

Background Information:
The Life and Spirituality of Julian of Norwich

Biography

The woman we have come to call Julian of Norwich (we do not know her real name) was born in Norwich, England, in 1342, most likely to an upper-class family. She was educated at a Benedictine convent and was better than most of her contemporaries at mastering literary skills, including the speaking and reading of French.

When Julian was thirty, she suffered a serious illness. During her illness, she received sixteen dramatic revelations of the love of God. She called those revelations showings, and she believed that they led her to become an anchoress.

To become an anchoress, a candidate had to meet with the bishop to show that her calling was sincere and that she had adequate means for support. After a special Mass, the anchoress would then live in a small room called an anchorhold, which was often built into the wall of a church. Here, she could see the altar and receive the Eucharist through a special opening. Julian's anchorhold was in the church Saint Julian's of Norwich, and she took its name when she became an anchoress.

Julian withdrew from society and devoted her life to prayer, contemplation, and counseling visitors from the window of her anchorhold. She wrote one work based on her sixteen revelations, titled *Showings*. She has been cited as the first English woman of letters and the first theologian to write originally in English. Some scholars have said that her book of medieval spiritual writings is profound and complex.

Julian lived a long time, but the exact date of her death is not known. She was named in a will in 1416, so we can assume that she was still alive at the age of seventy-four, which is amazing considering the frequent outbreaks of bubonic plague in England during that period.

Themes in Her Spiritual Writings

Images of God and the Trinity

Julian spoke of the Triune God as maker, protector, and lover. She also used both masculine and feminine images of God. Those themes are developed in her writing, where she makes this point about the Trinity:

> And so I saw that God rejoices that he is our Father, and God rejoices that he is our Mother, and God rejoices that he is our true spouse, and that our soul is his beloved wife. (*Showings,* p. 279)

References to maternal and feminine images of God are found in the Scriptures, and Julian applied them to Trinitarian relationships. In her interpretation, fatherhood meant power and goodness, and motherhood meant wisdom and lovingness. She presented the motherhood of God as a complement to the fatherhood of God.

Her writings about Jesus focus on his role as Christ the servant. It was through Christ that she reached God.

God's Unbounded Love for All Creation

Julian emphasized the ultimate worth of all of creation in God's eyes. Every human person has significance. Every acorn, every bird, every branch, every rock is created by God, loved by God, and protected by God. Her thinking was unusual in an atmosphere of anthropocentricity, that is, of considering human beings to be the most important entity of the universe and believing that everything else exists for their use (a viewpoint that is still dominant in Western culture today). Consider her words:

> [God] showed me something small, no bigger than a hazelnut, lying in the palm of my hand, as it seemed to me, and it was as round as a ball. I looked at it with the eye of my understanding and thought: What can this be? . . .

In this little thing I saw three properties. The first is that God made it, the second is that God loves it, the third is that God preserves it. But what did I see in it? It is that God is the Creator and the protector and the lover. (*Showings*, p. 183)

Optimism

Medieval life was marked by an obsession with sin, damnation, and death. Church teaching during the Middle Ages emphasized God's judgment, final damnation, and salvation. In contrast, Julian spoke of God's goodness, love, and mercy.

She struggled with those conflicting messages, and worked out a theology of sin and salvation that was faithful to her own experience of God, as shown in this passage:

And so our good Lord answered to all the questions and doubts which I could raise, saying most comfortingly: I may make all things well, and I can make all things well, and I shall make all things well, and I will make all things well; and you will see yourself that every kind of thing will be well. (*Showings*, p. 229)

Being Grounded in God's Word

Julian's book, *Showings,* is filled with biblical spirituality though she rarely quoted from the Bible. All that she wrote points to a profound knowledge of the scriptural text of the Latin Vulgate. The writings of Saint John and the letters of Paul are reflected in her work, but she was comfortable writing about God's revelation as she experienced, understood, and interpreted it. And for Julian, God's revelation was love. Consider this passage from her final chapter:

So I was taught that love is our Lord's meaning. And I saw very certainly in this and in everything that before God made us he loved us, which love was never abated and never will be. And in this love he has done all his works, and in this love he has made all things profitable to us, and in this love our life is everlasting. . . . In this love we have our beginning, and all this shall we see in God without end. (Pp. 342–343)

(The material in this section is quoted, adapted, and paraphrased from Gloria Durka, *Praying with Julian of Norwich,* pp. 15–23.)

Notes

Use this space to jot ideas, reminders, and additional resources.

Hildegard of Bingen

Overview

Hildegard of Bingen's world was filled with corruption, yet her response was to live justly and compassionately. She wanted to bring people back into harmony with the earth and all creation. Through her writing, preaching, and singing, Hildegard made a difference in her time and can inspire adolescent girls today.

Thematic Activities

Historical Context (45–60 minutes)

Preparation

○ Prepare to give the girls the background information on the biography of Hildegard of Bingen from the end of this chapter. Become familiar enough with the information that you can share it in a storytelling style. The material is taken from *Praying with Hildegard of Bingen,* by Gloria Durka (Winona, MN: Saint Mary's Press, 1991). It might be helpful for you to have a copy of that book for your own reference and enrichment.

1. Announce that the girls will be exploring the life and spirituality of a woman who, though she lived in the twelfth century, has much to say to them today. To begin with, you would like them to think about the time in which she lived.

Divide the girls into small groups, and give each group a large piece of poster board or newsprint and several markers. Direct the groups to write, "Twelfth century," in the middle of the paper. Ask them to think about what living in the twelfth century was like, and to add to the paper pictures, symbols, words, and phrases that describe the political, social, and church climate as they understand it. You might offer the following questions to help them focus their thoughts:

◈ What was it like to live as a teenage girl in medieval times?

◈ What were her prospects for the future?

2. Invite each group to share its completed poster and its thoughts about life in Hildegard's time. As each group presents, comment on its insights. If you notice any key themes developing, note them.

After all the groups have shared, summarize the information provided, noting or adding the following key points to round out the historical perspective:

- Kings united into countries lands that had been ruled by less powerful nobles. With those new nation-states, modern Europe was born.
- Towns and cities grew, complete with grand Gothic cathedrals and schools.
- Universities were founded, such as the Universities of Bologna and Oxford.
- Those who went against official church teachings were named heretics, and some were burned at the stake. The roots of the Inquisition were established.
- Many people died in the Crusades, so-called holy wars meant to take back the Holy Land from the Muslims.
- Confusion ravaged the church. In Hildegard's lifetime, thirteen popes and twelve antipopes claimed the chair of Peter.
- The rulers of the Roman Empire and the reigning popes frequently argued over matters of church and state.

3. Share the basic facts of Hildegard's life story with the girls. Invite the girls to close their eyes and imagine what Hildegard's life was like.

4. Lead a discussion of questions like the ones that follow, or invite the girls to write their answers to such questions:

- What did you find most interesting about Hildegard's life?
- What type of personality do you think Hildegard had?
- Hildegard had an incredible mentor in Jutta. Who are the mentors in your life? What are they like? What do you most admire about them?
- Hildegard's parents chose her mentor. If your parents were to choose a woman for you to learn from, who would they select and why?

Variation. Instead of presenting Hildegard's life story yourself, divide the girls into groups, and give each group a section of Hildegard's biography to tell or dramatize to the others. Provide costumes and props, or invite the girls to do so, if possible.

A Day in the Life of . . . (40–50 minutes)

This activity introduces monastic life and encourages the girls to incorporate into their own life some elements of a schedule centered around prayer.

1. Distribute handout 1, "A Typical Day in the Life of . . ." Give the girls a chance to fill in the information.

2. Distribute handout 2, "An Ideal Day in the Life of . . ." and ask the girls to complete it.

3. Divide the girls into pairs or small groups, and direct them to compare their typical and ideal days. You might encourage them to focus on questions like these:

- How close is your ideal day to your typical day?
- What changes would you have to make to get closer to an ideal day?
- Which of those changes are possible?

4. Distribute and review handout 3, "A Typical Day in Hildegard's Abbey." In particular, talk about the monastic trait of organizing one's life around prayer. Explain that the liturgy of the hours (also known as the Divine Office) is a series of gatherings of the community to chant the psalms, listen to the Scriptures, and sing hymns. Note that some of the hours are longer than others, with nocturn (or matins), laud, vespers, and compline being the most elaborate.

5. Lead a discussion of questions like these:

- Does anything about the schedule at Hildegard's abbey appeal to you? If so, what? What would challenge you?
- How does the daily routine promote a balanced, whole, and happy lifestyle?
- Are there any elements from Hildegard's routine that you would like to incorporate into your own schedule to make it more balanced? If so, which ones?
- What concrete steps could you take to bring together your typical day, your ideal schedule, and Hildegard's daily routine centered around prayer?

Variation 1. Instead of reading the daily schedule at Hildegard's abbey, lead the girls through a whirlwind 24-minute version of it. Designate one part of the meeting room as the chapel, one as the dining room, one as the work area, and so forth. Guide the girls from one part to the other, describing what the sisters would be doing at each place.

Variation 2. Play a recording of a group chanting the liturgy of the hours. In particular, give the girls an example of the psalmody, or the chanting of the psalms.

Music of the Soul (10–20 minutes)

Preparation

○ If possible, acquire a recording of Hildegard's music. Check libraries, online music services, and stores that sell medieval and Renaissance music.

1. Make the following comments in your own words. Then play a recording of Hildegard's music if you have one.

- Hildegard had great talent as a poet and composer. She believed that music was the highest form of praise to God. To her, singing was praying. She recognized music's power to touch the hearts and souls of people. She believed that music was not just a frill, but essential in the life of all people, rich and poor, because it touched their common humanity (Gloria Durka, *Praying with Hildegard of Bingen,* p. 91).

2. Lead a discussion of questions like the ones that follow, or give the girls an opportunity to write responses to such questions in their journal:

- ◉ How important is music in your life?
- ◉ What types of music stir your soul?
- ◉ Has a song ever moved you so much that you cried, prayed, or laughed? If so, describe that experience.
- ◉ Are there any "church" songs that really touch you or lead you to prayer? If so, what are they?
- ◉ Can a song change an attitude? If you answer yes, give an example.

3. Close with this prayer-poem written by Hildegard:

- ◉ "To the Trinity be praise!
    God is music, God is life
        that nurtures every creature in its kind.
    Our God is the song of the angel throng
        and the splendor of secret ways
        hid from all humankind,
    But God our life is the life of all."
                        (*Symphonia*, p. 143)

Variation 1. Explore music, literature, and art created by women through the ages. Have each girl choose a different composer, writer, or artist to research and present to the group.

Variation 2. Invite the girls to bring in recordings of songs that have touched them and to explain the songs' significance.

Variation 3. Create prayer cards or bookmarks with the text of Hildegard's prayer-poem, and give them to the girls.

Hildegard's Spiritual Legacy (40–60 minutes)

Preparation
○ Prepare to give the girls the background information on the spirituality of Hildegard of Bingen from the end of this chapter.

1. Present a summary of the characteristics of Hildegard's spiritual legacy.

2. Lead a discussion of this question: "Which of the five elements of Hildegard's spirituality do you think is the most important, and why?"

3. Divide the girls into five groups and assign each group a different one of the five elements. Challenge the groups each to develop a dramatic, musical, or visual expression of what their element means in the life of a teenage girl in the twenty-first century. Provide props and supplies, and allow adequate time for preparation and presentation.

Variation. Help the girls prepare a presentation and discussion that focus on Hildegard and women's spirituality. Invite mothers, grandmothers, and other women to participate in the program.

Just Like Jutta (35–50 minutes)

1. Review the story of the relationship between Hildegard and her mentor, Jutta, from the biography section of the background information at the end of this chapter.

2. Invite the girls to imagine themselves as mentors to younger girls in their school or community. Lead a discussion of questions similar to these:
- What advice would you pass on to the younger girls?
- What important lessons would you teach?
- What would you want the younger girls to know about God? about prayer? about religion?

3. Divide the girls into pairs or small groups. Give each pair or group a sheet of newsprint and markers. If the girls are in high school, ask them to list all the things a girl who is turning thirteen should know. If the girls are in middle school, ask them to list all the things a girl who is turning ten should know.

When they are finished, ask them to share their lists with everyone.

Variation 1. Compile the groups' lists into a master list, and have the girls send or deliver copies to girls who are turning ten or thirteen, along with an explanation of how the list was developed. The younger girls might be from the parish, a Girl Scout troop, a community group, or an elementary school.

Variation 2. Develop a mentoring service group for teenage girls and younger girls. Focus the meetings on topics that are of keen interest to girls, such as body image, relationships, prayer, and images of God.

Scriptural Connections

- Psalm 1 (Happy are those who delight in God.)
- Ps. 21:13 (We will sing and praise your power.)
- Matt. 5:14–16 (You are the light of the world.)
- John 15:16–17 (God chooses us. We do not choose God.)
- 1 Cor. 6:19–20 (Your body is the temple of the Holy Spirit.)

Background Information:
The Life and Spirituality of Hildegard of Bingen

Biography

Hildegard was born into a noble German family in 1098. When she was an infant, her parents dedicated her to God, as many devout parents did. When Hildegard was eight years old, her parents entrusted her to Jutta of Sponheim, a woman who lived in a hermitage next to a thriving monastery of men. Over time, Jutta grew to be not only Hildegard's mentor but her closest friend.

Jutta's reputation for wisdom and virtue drew women to join her, and her hermitage grew into a Benedictine monastery. Eventually, Hildegard entered the monastery and was educated in the Benedictine traditions of music, the sacred Scriptures, prayer, and work.

When Jutta died, Hildegard succeeded her as prioress. As the leader of the community, she was warm and strong, but also intense and determined. Many were drawn to Hildegard and the monastic way of life, and in time, she established other communities. Hildegard wanted her monasteries to be places of order and harmony, in contrast with the corrupt and chaotic medieval world.

Hildegard's reputation grew far beyond her land. Many people came to her for advice because she showed a keen awareness of the political and scholarly developments of her era. Hildegard was also known for her preaching. She had a deep spiritual awareness that was founded in what she named the reflection of the Living Light. She wrote nine books, dozens of poems, and nearly three hundred letters to nuns, kings, bishops, and nobles.

Legends tell that on 17 September 1179, two streams of light appeared in the sky and crossed over the room in which Hildegard was dying. That seems an appropriate accompaniment for the death of one nourished by the Living Light throughout her life.

Spiritual Legacy

Hildegard's spiritual writings focus on the following themes:
- *An ecological perspective.* She had a profound sense of being related to the earth. Unlike some of her contemporaries who rejected earthly life as binding their spirit, Hildegard believed that the earth was home and a region of delight, and as such must be admired, cherished, and protected.
- *A life of justice and compassion.* For Hildegard, being holy implied acting justly and doing good works. A lifestyle of good works requires awareness of the times, discernment of the good, choice as to course of action, and action itself.
- *A holistic use of our intelligence.* Hildegard's style of writing is fascinating and at times difficult, because she used an intricate array of metaphors and rich symbols. The wonderful images that she employed invite readers to taste and see the goodness of God. The writings of Hildegard prime our imagination and touch our intuition.

- *A mystical theology grounded in creation.* Hildegard experienced God living in and through all creation, but she did not collapse the identities of God and creation or dismiss their differences.
- *A woman true to her religious experience.* Hildegard reflected and wrote at length about the experience of women. Her correspondence reveals a lifestyle of political and social activism, and she regularly challenged the status quo.

(The material in this section is quoted, adapted, and paraphrased from Gloria Durka, *Praying with Hildegard of Bingen,* pp. 16–27.)

Notes

Use this space to jot ideas, reminders, and additional resources.

A Typical Day in the Life of . . .

What is a typical twenty-four-hour period like for you? Using this handout, plot your typical day. Include sleeping, eating, going to school, working, praying, playing, talking on the phone, watching television, and so forth.

6:00 a.m.

9:00 a.m.

12:00 noon

3:00 p.m.

6:00 p.m.

9:00 p.m.

12:00 midnight

3:00 a.m.

An Ideal Day in the Life of . . .

What would an ideal twenty-four-hour period be like for you? Using this handout, plot your ideal day, a day that would keep your life balanced, whole, and happy.

6:00 a.m.

9:00 a.m.

12:00 noon

3:00 p.m.

6:00 p.m.

9:00 p.m.

12:00 midnight

3:00 a.m.

A Typical Day in Hildegard's Abbey

The Benedictine way of life is well ordered, with a balanced rhythm of prayer, work, and study. Hildegard and her sisters worked about six hours, slept eight hours, prayed together three or four hours, and spent the rest of the day in spiritual reading, study, and meditation. All in all, the sisters aspired to live in harmony with God, humankind, and themselves.

2:00 a.m.
- chanting of *nocturn* (also called *matins*) with the community in the chapel
- back to sleep for a short time

6:00 a.m.
- chanting of *lauds* (now called morning prayer) with the community in the chapel
- private reading or meditation in one's own room
- more community prayer, this time known as *prime,* in the chapel
- a simple breakfast, followed by a brief period of morning work in the laundry, in the kitchen, or at housekeeping chores

9:00 a.m.
- chanting of *terce* with the community in the chapel, followed by a eucharistic liturgy
- another period of manual labor, this one in the herb garden, the vineyards, or the vestry (room where the garments and vessels used to celebrate the sacraments are stored and where the clergy dress)

12:00 noon
- chanting of *sext* with the community in the chapel
- lunch
- rest

3:00 p.m.
- chanting of *none* with the community in the chapel
- more work in the garden, the vestry, or the bakery

6:00 p.m.
- a light supper
- chanting of *vespers,* or evening prayer, with the community in the chapel
- private prayer, meditation, or spiritual reading

9:00 p.m.
- chanting of *compline* with the community in the chapel
- sleep

Foundresses of Religious Communities

Overview

Women have founded many religious communities throughout the centuries. They have often encountered obstacles in establishing their orders, and many have worked tirelessly setting up schools, hospitals, and places of prayer. Though the communities may share common threads, there is also often a great deal of diversity in their charisms. Adolescent girls can learn much from the strong women who created them, who dared to dream and left a distinct vision for those who followed.

This chapter contains four activities for exploring religious communities and the people involved in them. It is most suitable for girls in high school, though some middle school girls might enjoy the challenge of doing the suggested research.

Special Considerations

The girls will need access to the Internet to research Web sites of religious communities. If access is limited, contact your diocesan vocation office to see if it can provide information about the foundresses and communities you are interested in.

Thematic Activities

Monasticism and Women's Communities (40–55 minutes)

Preparation

○ From the list that follows, decide which foundresses you will offer the girls in step 2 of this activity. You might choose those who established communities represented in your area of the country, who established large communities, or who established small communities. List the names on the board.
  • Saint Madeleine Sophie Barat, *Society of the Sacred Heart of Jesus*
  • Saint Julie Billiart, *Sisters of Notre Dame de Namur*

- Saint Brigid, communities in Ireland
- Saint Frances Xavier Cabrini, Missionary Sisters of the Sacred Heart of Jesus
- Saint Clare of Assisi, Poor Clares
- Cornelia Connelly, Society of the Holy Child Jesus
- Saint Teresa de los Andes, Discalced Carmelites
- Saint Louise de Marillac, Daughters of Charity of Saint Vincent de Paul
- Saint Katharine Drexel, Sisters of the Blessed Sacrament
- Rose Hawthorne Lathrop, Servants of Relief for Incurable Cancer
- Blessed Catherine McAuley, Sisters of Mercy
- Saint Angela Merici, Order of Saint Ursula
- Saint Elizabeth Ann Seton, Sisters of Charity
- Saint Scholastica, Order of Saint Benedict
- others, perhaps with some connection to the religious communities in your area

1. Present a brief history of the monastic movement by making the following comments in your own words:

☯ Throughout the early centuries, men and women were drawn to a life of holiness, simplicity, and community. Their ideals often were at odds with the traditions of their world. Some of those men and women left the worldly ways of their society to pursue holiness and began the movement we call monasticism. Though *monasticism* literally means "dwelling alone," the movement had more to do with living apart from the masses.

☯ Monastic life began in the late third century. Inspired by Jesus, Moses, and the prophets who retreated to the desert to reflect on spiritual questions, the earliest monks and nuns lived alone, as hermits. Many were known as wise and holy people, and others sought them out. One of the earliest hermits was Anthony of Egypt, who moved to the desert around the year 270.

☯ A more communal vision of monastic life quickly took root, and in the fourth century, tens of thousands entered religious communities.

☯ Soon the need for guidelines became apparent. Basil, a monk and bishop in the fourth century, developed a rule of simplicity and obedience. Under his law, monks were to seek God in prayer, help the poor, care for the sick, and study. In later years, Saint Benedict founded a monastic order and established regulations that came to be known as the Rule of Saint Benedict.

☯ Many religious communities used similar guidelines to structure a simple, well-ordered, and balanced life. *Ora et labora,* Latin for "prayer and work," was the monastic way of life.

2. Ask the girls to choose one of the women you listed before the session, to research and present to the others. Explain that they may work individually or in small groups. Give each girl or group handout 4, "Foundresses," and tell everyone that their research should focus on the handout's questions.

The girls may find a good deal of information online. Many communities have Web sites for local communities, and most of those sites contain material on the order's values, mission, and foundress. The following general sites can be helpful starting places:

- *www.lcwr.org.* Leadership Conference of Women Religious.
- *www.catholic-forum.com.* Catholic Community Forum.
- *saints.catholic.org/index.shtml.* Catholic Online. This site provides an index of saints.
- *www.catholic-pages.com/dir/orders_women.asp.* This site includes links to many orders.

Allow each girl or group to choose a presentation format that they are comfortable with; some possible formats are listed below. You may want to set a time limit for the presentations.

- magazine article
- multimedia project
- oral report
- dramatization
- PowerPoint presentation
- news show interview, in the style of *Dateline* or *20/20*

3. Arrange for the girls to share their presentations, and lead a brief discussion after each presentation.

Praying with Strong Women (15–30 minutes)

Preparation
○ Set up a prayer table in your meeting space.

1. Give each girl an index card and assign her a woman from the list for the previous activity, "Monasticism and Women's Communities." Tell the girls to use the first person to write a short paragraph about this foundress, starting with, "I am."

2. Gather the girls in a circle around the prayer table. Call them, one by one, to read their "I am . . ." cards. After each reading, lead the group in saying, "Wise women, strong women, we wish to learn from you." Then invite the reader to add the card to the prayer table. Close with a few words of your own.

Community Charisms

1. Explain the concept charism to the girls by making the following comments in your own words:
- ◉ Each religious community was founded on key values known as its charism. A charism is a means to carry out a specific mission, a gift from God to a particular person or group in the church. All the members of a community embrace the charism, which directs their lifework.
- ◉ In many communities, generations of sisters have handed down special prayers, symbols, rituals, activities, and stories that illustrate and accompany their charism.

2. Divide the girls into small groups and assign each group a religious community of women that is active in or near your area. Explain that the groups are to complete the following tasks:

- Do some research on the community. Internet links and phone numbers should be available through your diocesan vocation office or the community's Web page.
- Arrange to interview, in person or by phone, one of the sisters to find out about the mission, charism, and history of the order. The girls might also invite the sister to visit the class.
- Prepare a brief presentation on the community's mission, charism, and history.

3. Invite the groups to share their presentations.

Becoming Foundresses (45–60 minutes)

1. Divide the girls into groups of three or four. Explain that each group will have a chance to found its own religious community of women. Ask the groups each to discuss questions like these:

- What needs in the world could use your attention, gifts, and talents?
- What issues do you feel strongly about?
- What type of religious order would you like to start to meet those needs and address those issues?
- What would be your order's charism, that is, key values?
- What rules or expectations would be part of your order?
- How would you attract people to work in your community?

Direct the groups each to create a charter—that is, a statement of purpose and mission that speaks to the charism of its order and outlines how the community members will live and serve. Give each group handout 5, "Community Charter," to use as a guide.

2. Call the groups to present their newly founded orders to one another. After each presentation, discuss questions like these:

- What appeals to you about the charter, the charism, and the rules of this community?
- What aspect of life in this community does not appeal to you?

3. Analyze the different needs and issues that the girls' communities deal with, and how those compare with the needs and issues that established religious orders serve today and have served throughout their history. Also discuss religious vocations and some of the issues facing many religious communities. You can find information on the latter topic in *Sisters: An Inside Look,* by Kathleen Rooney, in the Vocations series (Winona, MN: Saint Mary's Press, 2001).

Variation 1. Once their charter is determined and they have clearly identified the order that they are founding, give the groups tools to create a brochure that will invite others to join their community. They should make enough copies for everyone.

Encourage the use of art and the computer. Then hold a Religious Community Fair, at which the different groups pass out their brochures and recruit new members.

Variation 2. After the groups create their own community on paper, suggest that they search the Internet for the existing community that comes closest to their own ideals. Suggest that they contact the vocation director of that community for more information.

Options and Actions

- Invite representatives from religious communities of women in your diocese to speak to the girls about religious life, vocations, and so forth.
- Instruct the girls each to research the missions of ten communities online, and to identify the orders by mission category—education, health care, contemplative, missionary, outreach, and so forth. Combine everyone's results and review them as a group, noting how many communities are represented in each category. Ask the girls why more orders are dedicated in some areas than in others. Remind them that historically, most women were poor and uneducated.
- Read some of the recent research involving women religious and longevity, cancer, and health.

Scriptural Connections

- Matt. 28:16–20 (commissioning the disciples)
- Col. 3:12–17 (living as a Christian community)
- 2 Tim. 2:22–25 (leading a holy life)
- James 1:22–27 (ministering to others)
- 3 John, verses 5–8 (supporting ministers)

Notes

Use this space to jot ideas, reminders, and additional resources.

Foundresses

Develop a presentation on the foundress of the religious community of women you chose. Your research should focus around the following questions:

- Who was this woman? When and where was she born? What was her life like?

- What led her to a religious life?

- What was going on in the world when she founded her order?

- What was the purpose of founding the community? What is the mission statement of the order now?

- How did the order spread? In what parts of the world do the women serve now? How do they serve?

- How many women did the order start with? How many women were part of the community at its peak? How many women belong to the order now?

- What attracts women to the order? What is a typical profile of a new member?

- What issues does the community face at this time? How does it plan to deal with them?

- What was the most interesting thing that you learned in doing this research?

Community Charter

Who are we? (What is the name of our community?)

Why do we exist? (What is our core purpose?)

What is our charism? (What are our key values?)

What do we do? (What types of ministry do we perform?)

How do we do it? (What are our specific commitments, and how do we live them out?)

Saint Jane Frances de Chantal

Overview

Many of us desire to follow God but do not know how. Throughout her life, Jane Frances de Chantal faced challenges and pain, including the deaths of her mother, her husband, and two of her children. Saint Jane's life and mission tell how one woman faced reconciliation, adversity, and heartbreak, and was able to continually remain open to the Spirit's movement in her life. Like Saint Jane, we too can be true to God's plan for us, even when life does not play out exactly as we think it might.

The activities in this chapter are appropriate for girls in both middle school and high school.

Thematic Activities

A Woman of Favor, Fortune, Faith, and Forgiveness (40–55 minutes)

Preparation

○ Prepare to give the girls the background information on the mission and lifework of Saint Jane Frances de Chantal from the end of this chapter. You might also conduct an Internet search for additional biographical information.

○ Fill a bowl with four kinds of candy bars, one bar for each girl plus extras. Also set aside one bar of each kind, to distribute to the groups in step 3.

○ Obtain a blindfold.

1. Invite the girls to consider questions like these:
◉ Ten years ago, what did you think your life would be like at this point?
◉ In what ways is your life different from what you expected ten years ago? the same as what you expected?
◉ What do you think your life will be like five years from now?
◉ What do you think is God's plan for your life?

2. Provide a brief introduction on the life of Saint Jane, emphasizing the following points in your own words:

- The life of Saint Jane is the story of God's call to one woman. Jane has much to teach us about staying attuned to God's will.
- Like Jane, most of us seek to know God's will and wrestle with questions about it.
- Jane understood that the most important ingredient for knowing God's will is an intimate relationship with God.
- Our concern with knowing the will of God is not hard to understand. It springs from curiosity and a need for direction. On the deepest level, it reflects our desire to be accountable to God, and it speaks of a profound concern to accomplish something significant.
- The will of God is wrapped up not in the details of what we do but in the character of who we are. It is not just our large choices but also our daily small choices that build us into who God calls us to be.
- Our effort to gain insight on any important matter should be wholehearted. Like Saint Jane, we should seek the best information and guidance we can, consider it carefully, and allow time for our insights to season.
- God provides direction in every situation, even though we do not always recognize it. The Scriptures, prayer, reason, abilities, circumstances, desire, and the guidance of others can help us make tough decisions and give us confidence that we are following God's plan.

3. Ask a volunteer to leave the room for a few minutes. Once she has departed, divide the remaining girls into four approximately equal groups, and give each group a different kind of candy bar. Assign each group to a different part of the room, and tell the groups to hide their bar. When all the groups have done that, give the following instructions in your own words:

- Each group, in turn, will have 10 seconds to lead the volunteer to its candy bar. Group members can give any kinds of verbal clues, as long as they do not tell the volunteer what she is looking for or exactly where it is located. The search ends as soon as the volunteer finds one of the candy bars.

4. Bring the volunteer back into the room and blindfold her. Tell her that she is going on a search for something that will remain an unknown until she finds it. Explain that various people will tell her how to get to where she needs to go.

Conduct the activity until the volunteer finds a candy bar. You may, after a few rounds, allow the volunteer to choose just one of the groups to follow.

5. Remove the searcher's blindfold and ask her questions like the following ones:
- What are some words that describe what you felt during the search?
- What did you see, hear, or notice?

Then lead a discussion with the entire group, using questions like these:
- Have you ever felt the way the searcher did? If so, what was the situation?
- What factors got in the way of the searcher's finding a candy bar?
- What did you see, hear, or notice during the search?

6. Allow the girls each to choose a candy bar from the bowl you filled before the activity. Tell them to select one that they really like. While they are eating the candy, lead a discussion of questions like the ones that follow:

- ◉ How does it feel to choose something that you like?
- ◉ What situations in your life ask or demand that you make a choice?
- ◉ What would happen if you made a choice based solely on desire?
- ◉ What would happen if you made a choice based solely on what you think you should do because of obligation, peer pressure, authority, and so forth?
- ◉ What things get in the way when you search out God's will for you? What things do you have to go through to find God's will?

7. Make the following comments in your own words:

- ◉ Most of our options are not placed before us in a bowl, just begging for us to pluck one out.
- ◉ There are many different ways to live out God's will, just as there are many kinds of candy bars. We each have our own gifts, talents, and uniqueness, just as we each have our own favorite candy bar.
- ◉ Our goal is to find what we desire in our heart, and then use that to discover and follow God's will.

Spiritual Guides for Today (15–20 minutes)

1. Share the following comments in your own words:

- ◉ Through conversation with her spiritual guide, Saint Frances de Sales, Jane came to a deeper awareness of the presence and movement of God in her life. As she shared her dreams, struggles, triumphs, and fears, she became more open to God's will.

2. Ask the girls to define the term *spiritual guide*. Record their words and images on the board.

3. Invite the girls to name a person who is or could be a good spiritual guide or mentor for them. Lead them to identify the qualities they recognize in that person and to define the role a spiritual guide or mentor could play in their life. Be sure that the following information is incorporated into the discussion:

- ◉ Spiritual guides and mentors help us notice, savor, and respond to the movement of God in ordinary life. They are listening people who create an environment where we can look honestly at our relationship with God.
- ◉ Spiritual guides and mentors are found in every community of faith. They are people we come in contact with every day, like a grandmother, a young adult in the parish, a neighborhood couple, or a teacher.
- ◉ Spiritual guides do not always stand out as the most popular people or the ones who speak best.
- ◉ Spiritual guides are committed to living their faith and living according to Gospel values, day in and day out, and inspire us to do the same.

4. Urge the girls to write a letter to the person they named as a spiritual guide or mentor, highlighting the qualities they most admire in that person. Suggest that they send their completed letter.

Variation 1. Work with the girls to establish a spiritual mentoring program for young women at your parish or school. Initially, gather the girls and their mentors for prayer and discussion. Suggest that each girl and her mentor find a regular time every month or so to meet. Gather periodically as a group for check-in and enrichment.

Variation 2. Invite a spiritual director to speak to the girls about what the director does, who the director serves, what training the director has, and so forth.

Finding All the Pieces (20–25 minutes)

Preparation
○ Purchase or make small, blank jigsaw puzzles, one for every four to six girls. (You can simply cut the puzzles from index cards.)
○ Provide enough markers for everyone.

1. Create small groups of four to six people. Give each group a blank puzzle and enough markers for all the group members. Tell the groups to divide the puzzle pieces evenly among their members.

2. Share the following introduction with the girls:
◉ The Scriptures, prayer, reason, abilities, circumstances, desire, and the guidance of others are all tools that can help us make tough decisions and give us confidence that we are following God's plan.
◉ When we use all the methods available to us to learn what God's will is for us, things will often fit together like the pieces in a puzzle.

3. Direct the groups to brainstorm the key elements in their own lives that help them to discern God's will for them. Ask them to write each element on a separate puzzle piece.

4. Challenge the girls to come up with ways in which they have used or will use each element when they are puzzled about God's will for them. Offer an example, such as, "If the element is prayer, an action step might be to commit to regular or daily prayer."

5. Call the groups together and invite them to present their elements and actions to one another. Encourage each group to assemble its puzzle as it gives its presentation.

What Forgiveness Is, and Is Not (15–20 minutes)

1. Share the following information in your own words:

◉ The death of Jane's husband from a hunting accident offers a marvelous example of one woman's courage to forgive in the midst of pain and suffering. Many of us want to forgive. Like Saint Jane, we know from experience that forgiving feels better than hating and hurting. We want to express our generosity and compassion, but we do not fully understand what forgiveness is—and what it is not.

2. Create small groups of four to six girls, and give each group newsprint and markers. Explain that the groups should discuss their responses to the following two statements and then record those responses on the newsprint:

◉ Forgiveness is . . .
◉ Forgiveness is not . . .

3. Ask each group to share its responses with everyone. Then, in your own words, present the following ideas:

◉ Forgiveness is a choice. Asking the question, "Might I forgive?" puts the responsibility for action on us.

◉ Forgiveness is life-changing. Many of us believe that we cannot achieve happiness until someone comes crawling to us on their hands and knees, or learns their lesson, or promises to be different. But our happiness does not really depend on the behavior of other people. The forgiver changes her focus from "If only they would . . ." to "I wonder if I could . . ."

◉ Forgiveness is a skill. Like shooting basketballs through a hoop, it gets easier with practice. Some people recommend practicing first on the easy stuff: forgiving a grumpy teacher or an incompetent sales clerk. But sometimes the hard stuff becomes the training ground because it demands attention. Either way, the key, as with any skill-building process, is practice.

◉ Forgiveness does not mean forgetting. Forgiveness does not guarantee trust or reconciliation. After forgiving someone, we should not let ourselves continue to be abused, betrayed, used, or insulted. We can forgive and also say no.

◉ Forgiveness is empowering. Withholding forgiveness and nursing resentment simply allow another person to control our well-being.

4. Invite the girls to reflect on the following question, then solicit some of their responses: "How can you make forgiveness a more central part of your life?"

5. Make the following suggestions in your own words:

◉ Challenge the "shoulds" and "should nots" in your thinking. Forgiveness is much easier when you refuse to allow frustration, anger, and hostility to be fueled by the irrational expectation that other people will always act the way you want them to. Beware of the "shoulds" and "should nots" you hold on to, such as these:

- My mother should have known better.
- He should not have done this to me.

Whenever you find the phrase *should* or *should not* in your thoughts or speech, remind yourself that everyone is capable of making a mistake.

- Bury the grudge—literally. Write a letter to the person who hurt you, but do not mail it. Express fully, clearly, and honestly how you feel and why that person's act hurt you and made you angry. Conclude with the bold declaration that you have forgiven him or her. Then bury the letter somewhere in your yard or in a field far away.

Variation. Instead of having the girls discuss the sentence-starters in groups, distribute two index cards to each person, and ask everyone to write their own endings, one on each card. Then collect and redistribute the cards, and call the girls to take turns reading them aloud. (Consider using two colors of index cards, with one color assigned to each sentence-starter.)

Reconciliation Timeline (15–20 minutes)

1. Provide each girl with newsprint and markers, and invite everyone to create a timeline of key moments in their life. Offer a few suggestions, such as birth, Baptism, the first day of kindergarten, a special vacation, and the death of a grandparent. Give the girls an opportunity to share their finished timeline with a partner.

2. Ask the girls to go back to their timeline and mark two or three times when reconciliation was necessary, either because they had hurt someone or someone had hurt them. Encourage them to call to mind the feelings that were involved in each situation. Invite the girls to form small groups and, if they feel comfortable doing so, share one instance in which they were forgiven or offered forgiveness.

3. Discuss how forgiving and being forgiven help us become better followers of Jesus Christ.

Variation. Form small groups, and direct them each to write a prayer in honor of Saint Jane Frances de Chantal, asking God to bless them with the courage to forgive and to accept the forgiveness of others.

Prayer Service: An Affirmation of God's Call (5–10 minutes)

Gather the girls and encourage them to join you in the following prayer by responding, "I am," if they are willing to do what is asked:

- *Leader.* My friends, we are called by God to proclaim the Good News. In carrying out that call, we are God's witnesses to our friends, our families, our classmates, and our community, to one another. Like Saint Jane, our goal is to make God's life and love present in our world today. We conclude our time together, then, by reaffirming our commitment to living out this call. And so we pray together . . .

Leader. Our God has called us out of darkness into a wonderful light. Are you willing to continue to spread that light in your own individual way?

All. I am.

Leader. Our God has given each of us the gift of faith. Are you willing to share your faith and to witness to the truth of God's message, no matter how difficult?

All. I am.

Leader. Our God has given each of us abundant love and mercy. Are you willing to unite yourself more closely to Christ and to make Jesus the focal point of your daily living?

All. I am.

Leader. May the peace of God keep your hearts and minds in the knowledge and love of God, and of the Son, our Lord, Jesus Christ. May you be strengthened to carry out the ministry God has entrusted to you.

Invite the girls to offer one another a sign of peace and blessing.

Options and Actions

- Use resource 1, "In the Spirit of Saint Jane Frances de Chantal," to create pledge cards for the girls, and use them as part of a prayer service. Encourage the girls to sign their card and to use it as a daily reminder to strive to live out God's call.
- Conduct one of the following prayer services from the Voices manual *Prayer: Celebrating and Reflecting with Girls,* by Marilyn Kielbasa:
  - "God's Spirit Calling," pages 90–94 (on discernment)
  - "Healing the Brokenness: A Prayer for Peace and Reconciliation," pages 20–25
- Brainstorm with the girls additional action steps and projects that can promote forgiveness, reconciliation, and healing. Some examples:
  - Conduct a reconciliation service to seek and to receive pardon as individuals and as a community.
  - Find out about and participate in projects that promote peace among groups of people, such as the Ulster Project, a program dedicated to achieving peace between Catholics and Protestants in Ireland (information on this group can be found at *www.ulsterproject.org* or 262-786-8267).
- Highlight stories of forgiveness received, offered, or simply observed in your own community, by posting them in your parish or school newsletter, bulletin, or Web site. Or invite the girls to write their own stories of reconciliation or to research and write about the ways forgiveness is offered and lived out in the community.

- Celebrate International Forgiveness Day. Held the first Sunday of August, this event offers the opportunity for communities to honor and acknowledge individuals and organizations who are heroes of forgiveness. Contact the Worldwide Forgiveness Alliance at *www.forgivenessday.org* or 415-381-3372 for more information.

Scriptural Connections

- Gen. 33:1–17 (Jacob's meeting with Esau)
- Prov. 2:3–5 (trust in God)
- Jer. 29:11–14 (God's plan for us)
- Matt. 18:21–22 (forgiveness)

Background Information:
The Life and Spirituality of Saint Jane Frances de Chantal

Jane Frances de Chantal led a privileged life. She was born in France in 1572. Her father, a devout man, brought up Jane and her siblings after the death of her mother. At the age of twenty, Jane married.

Soon after Jane arrived at her new home, she discovered that she might lose it. Her husband, Christopher, had inherited the title *baron de Chantal*—and enormous debts as well. But Jane had not come to the marriage empty-handed. She had brought with her a deep faith instilled by her father, who had made daily religious discussion fun, allowing his children to talk about anything, even controversial topics. Her background helped the young Frenchwoman take charge by personally organizing and supervising every detail of the estate. Despite the early financial worries, she and her husband were devoted to each other and to their four children.

Jane's circumstances were altered dramatically when a hunting accident ended her husband's life. Before he died, her husband forgave the man who shot him. The heartbroken Jane, however, had to struggle with forgiveness for a long time. At first, she tried just greeting the man on the street. When she was able to do that, she invited him to her house. Finally, she was able to forgive him so completely that she even became godmother to his child.

Her husband's death left Jane grief stricken, a single parent, and at the mercy of a difficult father-in-law, who threatened to disinherit her children if she did not obey his smallest directive. Sometime after her loss, the young widow met Saint Francis de Sales, the bishop of Geneva. Jane had turned increasingly to God in her difficulty, and she found in Francis a wise and sensitive guide to the spiritual life. Jane's troubles opened her heart to her longing for God, and she sought God in prayer and in a deepening spiritual life. She spent many years discerning God's call for her.

In 1607, Francis enlisted Jane's help founding a religious order for women whose age or health prevented them from embracing the rigorous lifestyle of other religious communities. Jane believed that people should have a chance to live their calling regardless of their circumstances. Three years later, the first convent of the Daughters of the Visitation of Saint Mary was established, with Jane as director. In the following year, Jane opened more than eighty convents.

Saint Jane died on 13 December 1641 at the age of sixty-nine. Her feast day is celebrated 18 August.

Notes

Use this space to jot ideas, reminders, and additional resources.

In the Spirit
of Saint Jane Frances de Chantal

Inspired by the life, work, and mission of Saint Jane Frances de Chantal,
I pledge to do the following things:

PRAY each day.

FORGIVE others, and seek to be forgiven.

RENEW family relationships, particularly with family members who are difficult to love.

RESPECT life.

HONOR older people.

REACH OUT to those most in need, particularly those who are ill and suffering.

SMILE as a simple means of spreading God's love.

Inspired by the life, work, and mission of Saint Jane Frances de Chantal,
I pledge to do the following things:

PRAY each day.

FORGIVE others, and seek to be forgiven.

RENEW family relationships, particularly with family members who are difficult to love.

RESPECT life.

HONOR older people.

REACH OUT to those most in need, particularly those who are ill and suffering.

SMILE as a simple means of spreading God's love.

Inspired by the life, work, and mission of Saint Jane Frances de Chantal,
I pledge to do the following things:

PRAY each day.

FORGIVE others, and seek to be forgiven.

RENEW family relationships, particularly with family members who are difficult to love.

RESPECT life.

HONOR older people.

REACH OUT to those most in need, particularly those who are ill and suffering.

SMILE as a simple means of spreading God's love.

Blessed Kateri Tekakwitha

Overview

Blessed Kateri Tekakwitha's life was ordinary in many ways, but it was extraordinary because of the qualities she embodied. Kateri experienced much pain, sorrow, and hardship. Yet, in all things, she found joy and peace through belief in Jesus Christ. The lessons of Kateri's life offer the girls an opportunity to explore their own life and faith commitments. As the patron of ecology, Kateri has much to teach them about commitment to and working for the environment as well.

The activities in this chapter are appropriate for girls in both middle school and high school.

Thematic Activities

The Patron Saint of Ecology (40–55 minutes)

This activity invites the girls to connect with a single environmental issue and to develop a strategy to acquire support for that problem within their community. The girls have an opportunity to learn a few facts about the issue, but the main task is to convince one another that they should be committed to helping solve the problem.

Preparation
○ Prepare to give the girls the background information on the mission and lifework of Blessed Kateri Tekakwitha from the end of this chapter. Consider obtaining a copy of *Kateri Tekakwitha: Mystic of the Wilderness*, by Margaret R. Bunson (Huntington, IN: Our Sunday Visitor, 1998), and searching the Internet, for additional biographical information.
○ Review your local newspaper or contact an environmental advocacy group, to determine what issues are most pressing in your community at this time. Be sure to have some basic information about those issues available for the girls to review.
○ Gather a variety of creative supplies, including paper, markers, and pens.

1. Provide a brief introduction on the life of Blessed Kateri Tekakwitha, or ask one of the girls to do some research and present the material. Be sure that the following points are included in the introduction:

- ❧ Kateri, known as the Lily of the Mohawks, was a woman of conviction. A lesser person might well have yielded to the pressure to abandon her pursuit of God. But Kateri was not to be dissuaded.
- ❧ The Mohawks were known as the people of the woodlands. Because they were close to the earth and dependent on the environment, they considered all living things sacred. From the animals of the forest, the birds of the air, and even the rocks in the field, they drew the message that the Great Spirit was in charge of the universe.
- ❧ This reverence for nature and the influence of her mother planted in Kateri a yearning to build quality of character in her people. Kateri, the patron saint of ecology, was a living example of determination and fortitude.

2. Invite the girls to brainstorm current environmental issues, especially ones that concern your community. You might begin by offering a few suggestions. List the issues on the board as the girls name them.

3. Break the girls into groups of four to six. Direct the groups each to choose one of the issues identified in the brainstorming and to come up with reasons why people should really care about it. Invite each group to develop a brief presentation about its issue, using one of the following four formats, and provide the instructions for these formats in your own words:

- ❧ *Television announcement.* Develop a short skit that expresses why people should support your cause. If you have access to a video camera, you might tape the skit. Television is a visual medium, so pictures, graphs, and props would be good resources.
- ❧ *Radio announcement.* Develop a 1-minute announcement that vividly expresses your issue. If you have a tape recorder, make a tape of the announcement. People won't be able to see you during the announcement, so you will need to use sound to convince them that your issue is important.
- ❧ *Letter to the editor or cartoon.* Write a letter to the editor, or create a cartoon, that tells the story behind your issue. You do not have the luxury of using sound, so your words and pictures must be vivid.
- ❧ *Web page.* Create a Web page that supports your issue.

4. Invite each group to give its presentation. Then lead a discussion using questions like these:

- ❧ Why is it important that other people hear and act on these messages?
- ❧ Do you think your message was accepted by the entire group?
- ❧ If it was not accepted, how do you feel? If it was accepted, how would you have felt if it had not been? Can rejection change your dedication or commitment to the cause?
- ❧ Why, do you think, was it important for Kateri to stand firm in her beliefs?
- ❧ What characteristics does Kateri model for girls and women in today's world?

Variation 1. After all the presentations have been made, give each girl a small piece of paper. Tell everyone to write on their paper the two issues that they feel are the most important of those explored. Tally the results and use them in the concluding discussion.

Variation 2. Invite the girls to brainstorm ways that their community can help the environment. From their ideas, choose six that are practical and that young children and older people could easily accomplish. Publish those six ideas in your parish bulletin or school newsletter.

Fortitude Defined (20–30 minutes)

1. Share the following introduction in your own words:
   ◉ Fortitude consists of strength of mind that enables a person to meet danger or bear pain or adversity with courage. Kateri was a model of fortitude. This activity provides an opportunity to define fortitude for yourself and to share your own stories of courage.

2. Divide the girls into groups of four to six. Provide them with newsprint and markers. Ask them to write words or images that come to mind when they hear the word *fortitude.* Then invite the groups to share their responses with everyone. (Note: This is not a common word for some girls. You might suggest that the young women use a thesaurus if they have trouble coming up with responses.)

3. Encourage the girls to get into a comfortable position for reflection. Present the following sentence-starters, pausing after each one to give the girls a chance to reflect:
   ◉ A time when I stood up for what I believed was . . .
   ◉ It takes courage for me to . . .
   ◉ I am most proud of myself when I . . .

4. Invite the girls to share their stories of strength and courage with their small groups.

5. Lead a discussion of ways the young women can support and encourage one another in being strong and courageous. Action steps might include these:
- Send a note of affirmation.
- Publicly acknowledge an accomplishment.
- Speak out on one another's behalf.
- Pray for one another daily.
- Start a girl's group for support and discussion.

Variation. View the musical drama *The Lily,* by Jim Davis, which tells the story of Kateri's life. Follow the viewing with a group discussion. You can purchase a copy of the musical from PublicReports.com at *www.publicreports.com/thelily/index.htm* or 707-429-4256.

The Reality of the Cross (15–20 minutes)

Preparation
○ Gather sticks, two for each girl.
○ Bring in a ball of twine or yarn.
○ Create a sample cross by using twine or yarn to fasten two crossed sticks at the point of intersection.

1. Share with the girls the following information, in your own words:
   - Kateri experienced difficulties, including being orphaned in childhood; enduring a lifetime of ill health; being ridiculed, scorned, and rejected by her foster parents and fellow villagers; leaving her homeland; and suffering the anguish of the illness that took her life.
   - She accepted those trials patiently and bore them with love. Kateri did not allow those crosses to discourage or defeat her, but saw in them an opportunity for growth and an inspiration to work quietly and selflessly to alleviate the pain and suffering of others.
   - Her favorite devotion was to fashion crosses out of sticks and place them throughout the woods. Those crosses served as stations that reminded her to spend a moment in prayer. This activity invites you to do the same.

2. Distribute two sticks and a piece of twine or yarn to each girl. Show your sample and tell the girls to simply tie their sticks together to make a cross.

3. Gather the girls in a circle with their crosses. Invite them to silently call to mind people who are suffering, experiencing loss or rejection, or ill. After a few moments, invite them to say aloud together, "May the people we are thinking about have the strength of Kateri in carrying their cross."

Variation 1. Instead of gathering the sticks yourself, take the girls outdoors and direct them to gather their own. You might even do the entire activity outdoors.

Variation 2. Construct wooden stations of the cross on the parish or school grounds or at a local retreat center. Invite those who attend the facility to use the stations for the traditional devotion or as reminders to offer prayers for courage and fortitude.

A Litany for Kateri Tekakwitha (10 minutes)

1. Make the following comments in your own words:
   - Kateri was a woman of great prayer and a woman who had a deep awareness of God's love for her. How else but through her life of prayer can we explain her extraordinary faith response?
   - Just as prayer was a key to Kateri's life, it must also be the foundation of our life, however hectic that life may be.

2. Distribute handout 6, "A Litany for Kateri Tekakwitha." Lead the girls in reciting the litany.

Options and Actions

- Celebrate the feast day of Kateri Tekakwitha on 14 July, by organizing an outdoor prayer service about caring for the earth.
- Begin a prayer group to pray for the canonization of Blessed Kateri Tekakwitha. For more information about the canonization process or to obtain novenas and prayers, contact the Blessed Kateri Tekakwitha League at *www.kateritekakwitha.org/kateri/ league.htm* or 518-853-3153.

Scriptural Connections

- Ps. 95:4–5 (God made the land.)
- Isa. 12:2 (God is my strength.)
- Jer. 31:3 (God is faithful.)
- Dan. 3:57–82 (Blessings come from the earth.)
- John 14:27 (Do not be afraid.)

Background Information:
The Life and Spirituality of Blessed Kateri Tekakwitha

Kateri Tekakwitha was born near Auriesville, New York, in 1656, the daughter of a Mohawk warrior. When she was four years old, smallpox spread through the Mohawk nation. Kateri was the only member of her family to survive, although the disease left her with a scarred face and poor vision. The little girl was adopted by her aunt and her uncle, the new chief.

Although Kateri had not been baptized as an infant, she had fond memories of her prayerful Christian mother and of the stories of Christian faith that her mother had shared with her in childhood. Those remained indelibly impressed on her mind and heart and gave shape and direction to her life.

When Kateri was twenty, French Jesuit missionaries came to Caughnawaga, the village where she lived in Quebec, Canada. Perhaps inspired by memories of her mother, and moved by the words of the priests, Kateri wished to convert to Christianity. Her uncle was opposed to the new religion, however, and the shy, obedient young woman did not approach the missionaries.

One afternoon, Father de Lamberville paused outside a cabin where Kateri was recovering from a foot injury. The young Mohawk girl was overjoyed to see the missionary and quickly told him how greatly she desired to become a Christian, no matter what the obstacles. She soon began religious instruction, and on Easter Sunday, she was baptized. She was given the name Catherine, or in Mohawk, Kateri (before Baptism, she had been called Kehenta).

After her conversion, Kateri became the victim of relentless persecution in her village. As she walked to the mission chapel, children and drunk people hurled mud, stones, and insults. Her life was threatened if she did not renounce her new religion. Though she worked harder than ever during the week, her aunts refused her food because she would not work on Sunday. Through all of this, Kateri remained steadfast.

In July 1677, Kateri left her village and fled 200 miles through woods, rivers, and swamps to the Christian Indian mission of Saint Francis Xavier, near Montreal. Kateri's journey through the wilderness took more than two months. She joyously received her first Communion a few months after her arrival.

Although uneducated and unable to read and write, Kateri led a life of prayer and penitence. She taught young people and cared for sick and older people. Her favorite devotion was to fashion crosses out of sticks and place them throughout the woods. Those crosses served as stations that reminded her to spend a moment in prayer. She was devoted to the Eucharist and to Jesus Crucified.

Kateri Tekakwitha spent almost four years at the mission. There, her faith flourished, but her always frail health failed. She died on Wednesday of Holy Week, 17 April 1680. Her last words were, "Jesus, I love you."

Fifteen minutes after her death, the priest at her bedside saw an extraordinary change come over her. The smallpox scars that had marred her thin features vanished, and her face became radiant and beautiful.

Devotion to the saintly Mohawk girl began almost at once. Wonderful cures happened when her name was invoked or through the use of her relics or dust from her grave. Novenas and Masses were offered in her honor, not only by the Indians but by white settlers as well.

In 1943, she was declared venerable. In 1980, she was beatified. She is now one step away from sainthood. She is the first Native American and the first American laywoman to be honored this way.

Notes

Use this space to jot ideas, reminders, and additional resources.

A Litany for Kateri Tekakwitha

Kateri, loving child of God and Lily of the Mohawks, we thank God for the many graces you were given. Help us to be more like you in love for God and for people.

> Kateri, bright light for all Indians, pray for us.
> Kateri, courage of the afflicted, pray for us.
> Kateri, lover of the cross of Jesus, pray for us.
> Kateri, unshakeable in temptations, pray for us.
> Kateri, full of patience in suffering, pray for us.
> Kateri, lover of penance, pray for us.
> Kateri, who traveled many miles to learn the faith, pray for us.
> Kateri, steadfast in all prayer, pray for us.
> Kateri, example to your people in all virtues, pray for us.
> Kateri, humble servant to the sick, pray for us.
> Kateri, your holy death gave strength to all Indians . . . pray for us.
> Kateri, whose scarred face in life became beautiful after death, pray for us.
> (Excerpted from Doris Staton, "Litany of Kateri Tekakwitha," originally appearing in *Lily*, winter 1987, as quoted at *www.kateritekakwitha.org/kateri/litany.htm*, accessed 26 September 2001.)

Blessed Kateri Tekakwitha, pray for us.

May we who honor Kateri be truly enriched, uplifted, and renewed by the example of this humble Indian girl, the Lily of the Mohawks.

Amen.

Saint Teresa of Ávila

Overview

Teresa of Ávila wrote books at a time when most women could not read or write. She also taught the sisters in her convent about prayer at a time when women were forbidden to teach about God or religion. Her book *The Interior Castle* describes the growth of the soul as it journeys through seven rooms of a castle. Though her writings were challenged by many people, simply because she was a woman, church authorities eventually recognized her profound wisdom and named her a saint, and later, a doctor of the church.

The first seven activities in this chapter are designed to help you lead high school girls on a journey of self-discovery through their own interior castle. In the seven rooms of their castle, they have the opportunity to sort out and make sense of their own experiences as situations grounded in their relationship with God.

Special Considerations

Unlike the other activities in this manual, which are generally independent of one another, the activities in this chapter should be done consecutively. The format for the first seven activities is the same: dressing the prayer table, a narrative on Teresa's life and description of the theme, discussion questions and exercises, and a short closing prayer. Also included in the chapter is a final prayer service.

The repetitive and reflective nature of the activities provides an experience that the girls may not be accustomed to. Assure them that those who enter into each situation with an open mind and heart will discover many riches within themselves.

The series of activities lends itself to a retreat format for older girls, though the rooms can also be visited one at a time over several days or weeks. The activities are best done with a small group. However, they can be adapted for use with as many as thirty girls, providing all the participants enter the experience willingly.

Thematic Activities

Preparation

○ Prepare to give the girls the background information on Teresa of Ávila from the end of this chapter.

○ For the prayer space, provide items that can increase the girls' awareness of the sacred, such as cloth, a crucifix or icon, a Bible, flowers, stones, and seashells.

○ Invite each girl to bring a special candle, preferably one that is of a distinctive shape and color. Or purchase a variety of candles and have the girls choose one during the first session.

○ Some of the exercises involve reflection and writing. You may want to suggest that the girls bring their own journal for this purpose.

○ Write the closing prayer for each activity on a separate sheet of poster board or newsprint.

Room 1: What's in a Name? (30–60 minutes)

1. Offer a brief introduction to the life of Teresa of Ávila. Do not feel as if you must give all the background information in the first activity; pieces of Teresa's biography are part of every activity.

2. Set up a prayer space with the girls by covering a small table with cloth and placing on it a variety of objects that may be a source of reflection. Direct the girls to place their candles on the table. Light the candles and keep them lit throughout the activity.

3. Read or summarize the following narrative:

◉ Teresa de Ahumada y Cepeda was born in Ávila, Spain, on 28 March 1515. Ahumada was the last name of her mother, Beatriz. Cepeda was the last name of her father, Alonzo, who had received it from his mother.

In many cultures, children carry the names of both mother and father so that the families of both will be long remembered and honored. Today, it is not uncommon for married women to retain their identify by using both their own family name and their husband's, connected with a hyphen, as in Joanne Anderson-Smith.

Teresa went through many name changes that reflected the changes in her life circumstances. As a teenager, she dropped her father's name and was known as Teresa Ahumada. As a nun, she became known as Sister Teresa of Jesus. As a saint, she is called Saint Teresa of Ávila, doctor of the church.

4. Lead the girls in a discussion of questions like the ones that follow:

◉ What is the last name of your mother's family? How is her maiden name being continued in the family?

◉ When you were baptized, what name were you given?

◉ Are you named after someone special, such as a family member? a friend? a saint?

⊚ Does your name have a special meaning?

⊚ What is your Confirmation name? Why did you choose it?

⊚ What nicknames are you known by? Who gave those to you? What do they say about you, about how others see you, and about how you view yourself?

⊚ Do you carry a title or special name in any organization that you belong to? For example, are you a cocaptain of the volleyball team? a senior Girl Scout? a forward on your soccer team? the second-chair clarinet in the band? the favorite baby-sitter for a neighborhood family?

5. Distribute small pieces of paper. Tell the girls to write their full name on their piece of paper, with all the titles they carry. Then call each person to read her name aloud in turn, slowly and prayerfully.

6. Invite the girls to sit quietly with their name for about a minute, focusing on its power to identify them and their special place in the universe. Then display the closing prayer and lead the group as it slowly repeats the prayer three times:

God, you see me and you know me.
You have called me by name.
I am yours.

Room 2: Love God and Love One Another (30–60 minutes)

1. Set up a prayer space with the girls as you did when the group visited the first room. Invite the girls to light their candles.

2. Read or summarize the following narrative:

⊚ Teresa's parents were *conversos,* that is, Jews who had converted to Christianity. At that time, Jews suffered persecution and were being expelled from Spain because of their faith.

When Teresa's father was young, he and his father were paraded naked through the streets of Toledo to experience disgrace. His family, although Christian, were suspected of secretly practicing the Jewish faith. Their possessions were confiscated and they were confined to their homes in social disgrace and dishonor.

3. Lead the girls in a discussion of questions like these:

⊚ When have you felt that you were a victim of injustice? How did it make you feel? How did you handle the situation? If a similar incident occurred today, what would you do differently?

⊚ In what situations are people treated unfairly, unjustly, or unequally in your school? in your community? in the world?

⊚ What do the Scriptures say about treating others with love and compassion? What specific verses address that issue?

◎ When you see others being treated unfairly or excluded from social groups, what do you do? Describe a time when you acted on behalf of someone who was being mistreated.

4. Invite the girls to close their eyes and sit quietly for about a minute with all that has been revealed. Then display the closing prayer and lead the group as it slowly repeats the prayer three times:

God of justice, you equally welcome everyone into your presence and love. Teach us your way.

Room 3: Learn from One Another (30–60 minutes)

1. Set up a prayer space with the girls as you did when the group visited the first room. Invite the girls to light their candles.

2. Read or summarize the following narrative:

◎ By the time Teresa was born, her father, Alonzo Sanchez de Cepeda, was well known as a devout Catholic and a wealthy businessman. Her mother, Beatriz de Ahumada, had married at the age of fifteen and borne ten children. The family also included two children from Alonzo's previous marriage (his first wife had died).

Beatriz was described as frail and sickly, and she and the children seldom left their home or entertained. The children played in the courtyard gardens. Teresa and her brother Lorenzo pretended to be martyrs for Jesus Christ and the faith. One day, they even ran away together to join the Crusades. However, they quickly abandoned their plan.

Probably because of the many years she had spent in the family gardens, Teresa described Jesus Christ as a gardener who watered the thirsty soil of the soul in prayer. Clean water was precious in those days, so it was used only for specific purposes: cleansing, satisfying thirst, and Baptism.

3. Lead the girls in a discussion of the following question: "God is called by many names: Gardener, Shepherd, Mother Eagle, and Judge, to name a few. What name or image best describes God for you?"

4. Read the story of Mary of Magdala's visit to the tomb of the risen Jesus, when she thought he was the gardener, in John 20:11–18. Distribute paper or ask the girls to use their own journals. Repeat the two questions that Jesus asked Mary:

◎ "Why are you weeping?"
◎ "Who are you looking for?"

Suggest that the girls spend 10 minutes or so writing their answer to Jesus, as if he had asked the questions of them today.

5. Assign each girl a partner—or spiritual companion—or let the girls choose their own. Allow time for the spiritual companions to share whatever is comfortable for them from their answers to Jesus' two questions. Ask them to include in their sharing some discussion of the following question: "Just as Mary of Magdala proclaimed the news of Jesus' Resurrection to the Apostles, what good news do you proclaim as a disciple of Jesus'?"

6. Invite the girls to close their eyes and sit quietly for about a minute with all that has been revealed. Then display the closing prayer and lead the group as it slowly repeats the prayer three times:

God of many names, you are a friend who is always with us.

Room 4: Our Mothers, Our Selves (30–60 minutes)

1. Set up a prayer space with the girls as you did when the group visited the first room. Invite the girls to light their candles.

2. Read or summarize the following narrative:
◉ Teresa and her mother had a close relationship. When Teresa was young, they would read romance novels together and dream of adventures in faraway countries. Beatriz was frequently ill and seldom left her room, but she used her imagination to go beyond the boundaries of the house and into the excitement and thrills of other times and places.

Through her relationship with her mother, Teresa learned that her imagination could teach her a lot about herself and open the world to her. She believed that many of the possibilities that she imagined could become realities.

Teresa spent much time alone, reading and praying. She began to look inward to experience God. She imagined the soul as a rich palace, built entirely of gold and precious stones, with God sitting in the center. She felt that the closer a person could come to the center of the soul, the brighter would be the light to see God and realize the wonder of being human.

3. Lead the girls in a discussion of questions similar to the ones that follow:
◉ Describe some one-on-one times that you have had with your mother, a grandmother, an aunt, or an older female friend. What have you learned from those times? How have they made you feel?
◉ When is the best time for you to be alone? What happens when you are alone?
◉ Have you ever experienced a sudden insight during times of quiet? If so, describe your insight.

4. Invite the girls to close their eyes and sit quietly for about a minute with the image of their soul as a palace built entirely of gold and precious stones. Then display the closing prayer and lead the group as it slowly repeats the prayer three times:

God, like a mother, you feed me with your wisdom and love me like your special child.

Room 5: The Voyage into the Unknown (30–60 minutes)

1. Set up a prayer space with the girls as you did when the group visited the first room. Invite the girls to light their candles.

2. Read or summarize the following narrative:

⊚ When Teresa was thirteen years old, her mother died. Most of Teresa's brothers had left home to explore new lands. Without her mother and brothers as companions, Teresa's whole world was suddenly changed. Besides that, her body was taking on a different shape, and she was approaching the age when most respectable girls either married or entered a convent.

At sixteen, Teresa was sent to a convent school, perhaps to keep her away from a young man of whom her father did not approve. While away, Teresa began to search and discover the exciting, unending, and powerful inner world of her soul, through prayer and reading—two things she had learned to do with her family.

Through her kinship with others, Teresa learned many things that later helped her to know that the soul does not grow in the same way and at the same rate as the physical body. Some children have a mature soul, whereas many adult souls have not been open to the care of the Divine Gardener, who tends to them through prayer.

3. Lead the girls in a discussion of questions such as these:

⊚ How has life changed for you in the past year or two?
⊚ What about you is most like your mother? your father? another significant adult in your life?
⊚ What other personal gifts have helped you to be who you are today?
⊚ How do you influence or shape the mind and soul of other people?

4. Assign each girl a partner or ask the girls to choose their own spiritual companion. Pose questions like the following ones for discussion:

⊚ Do you pray? If so, why, when, and how?
⊚ When and how have your prayers been answered?
⊚ What would you like your prayer life to be like?
⊚ How can you and your partner help each other develop your prayer life during the next month?

5. Invite the girls to close their eyes and sit quietly for about a minute with all that has been revealed. Then display the closing prayer and lead the group as it slowly repeats the prayer three times:

Glory and praise to God in the highest. Your work is marvelous to me.

Room 6: Becoming Who We Are Created to Be (30–60 minutes)

1. Set up a prayer space with the girls as you did when the group visited the first room. Invite the girls to light their candles.

2. Read or summarize the following narrative:

❧ While other people restricted their prayer life to set formulas that they memorized, Teresa silently spoke to God from her heart. In those times of prayer, she thought only of God, and she spoke to God as she would a close friend or family member. She always remembered that prayer had the power to make people more aware of and attentive to the changes in their life. In fact, she compared prayer to a silkworm enclosing itself in a cocoon, in which the silkworm is eventually transformed into a moth.

Teresa's advice to her "daughters" is to remember that the God they pray to is present within them. She also reminds them that they must listen very carefully to how God responds.

3. Lead the girls in a discussion of questions such as these: "Teresa compared prayer to a silkworm enclosing itself in a cocoon, to eventually be transformed into a moth. Does this image work for you? What other images of prayer come to mind?"

4. Ask the girls to lie on the floor or assume some other comfortable position, and close their eyes. Make the following comments and invitation in your own words:

❧ You know that God has responded to your prayer if you feel refreshed, if you feel at peace, if you have a more positive outlook, or if you feel like doing good things for other people or creation.

❧ Remain quiet for a few minutes. Let your heart speak to the heart of God. Then sit in silence for a few more minutes and let God speak to your heart.

5. Invite the girls to close their eyes and sit quietly for about a minute with all that has been revealed. Encourage them to be aware of and attentive to the voice of God throughout their day, and to review the action of God in their day before going to bed at night. Then display the closing prayer and lead the group as it slowly repeats the prayer three times:

Day and night, you are with me.
Day and night, you are here.

Room 7: Being All That We Can Be (30–60 minutes)

1. Set up a prayer space with the girls as you did when the group visited the first room. Invite the girls to light their candles.

2. Read or summarize the following narrative:

❧ Teresa taught other women about the freedom and the wisdom she found in prayer. She wrote a book about prayer, which she called *The Way to Perfection*. She also wrote several other books that many people still read to gain a better understanding of how to form a close kinship with God.

In Teresa's day, women were not allowed to teach and write books on religious matters. She was questioned by the church, and her books were banned in many places. With God's grace and the encouragement of others, she continued to write and teach, although doing so exposed her to many dangers.

Teresa's first book was an autobiography titled *The Book of Her Life.* Reading her autobiography is like peering into her soul and seeing the spirit of a person who tore down many social and religious barriers for women in her day. For example, when Teresa entered the convent, the nuns who were from rich families were separated from everyone else and enjoyed many privileges and advantages denied the others. Prayer and self-examination led Teresa to establish convents where all women were welcome and were treated equitably. Prayer was the center of life in her convents, and everyone was treated as precious in God's eyes.

3. Announce that the girls will begin to write their own spiritual autobiography, just as Teresa did. They can start at any point in their life. Suggest that they first create an outline, and then work on their autobiography over the next few weeks. Explain that by writing this personal history, they can gain a deeper knowledge about themselves in relationship to God and all creation.

You might suggest the following questions, or others, as springboards for their writing:

◉ When did you first become aware of God in your life?

◉ How did you arrive where you are today in your spiritual journey?

◉ Where do you want to go, spiritually?

◉ What have you accomplished?

◉ What do you want to do in the future?

◉ How are you being prepared now for what will happen in the future?

◉ What does God say to you about fairness and justice? about love and compassion?

◉ How have you learned to trust God? What makes it difficult to do so?

4. Invite the girls to close their eyes and sit quietly for about a minute with all that has been revealed. Then display the closing prayer and lead the group as it slowly repeats the prayer three times:

All things are changing.
Only God remains the same.
Those who possess God want for nothing.
God alone suffices.

Variation. Combine the exploration of this room with the spiritual autobiography retreat "Sacred Journeys," on pages 43–56 in the Voices manual *Retreats: Deepening the Spirituality of Girls,* by Julia Ann Keller. Adapt the retreat to use the autobiography of Teresa of Ávila instead of Dorothy Day.

Prayer Service: The Awakening of the Soul (15–25 minutes)

Preparation

○ Add to the prayer space an evergreen branch and a clear bowl filled with water.

○ Prepare a short reflection on the events that have transpired during your group's pilgrimage through the interior castle.

○ Choose a song about walking with God that all the girls might know, and provide copies of it.

1. Gather the girls around the prayer table and have each light her candle. Read Isa. 43:1–2,4–5, commenting that this passage reflects what occurred in the exploration of the seven rooms of the interior castle with Saint Teresa.

2. Dip the evergreen branch in the bowl of water and sprinkle each girl in a gesture of blessing.

3. Share your reflection on the journey that the girls experienced together. You may want to highlight the following points:

◈ We have dwelled in the seven rooms of our interior castle through the experience, soul, and spirit of Teresa of Ávila, in search of God and our true self.

◈ In each room, we have opened our soul to be watered by God so that it can grow closer to the divine Source of all light and life.

◈ We have learned from Teresa about the importance of prayer, trusting in God, paying attention to God's revelation in unusual times and places, and the role that others play in our spiritual growth.

Invite the girls to share their own insights and reflections on their journey.

4. Call each girl by name and ask her to hold her candle. Lay your hands on her head as you repeat her name and say something like the following: "You are richly blessed and deeply loved by God for all eternity."

5. Close with the song you chose before the activity. Invite the girls to share a sign of peace.

Options and Actions

• Before visiting the first room, have the girls create their own special candles. Make sure each girl has a plain pillar candle, and provide a variety of used magazines, scissors, and paintbrushes, and a decoupage coating such as Mod-Podge. Tell the girls to cut out words and pictures that represent God to them, or any other theme that you choose. You may also want to have them cut out letters and spell their name. Direct them to attach all the clippings to their candle with Mod-Podge, and then paint a thin coat of Mod-Podge over the entire candle.

- Designate different girls to find a symbol for each room of the castle. Add those symbols to the prayer space. For example, a book of baby names could serve as a symbol for room 1, and a Mother's Day card for room 4.
- Put the closing prayers on separate small cards and distribute them to the girls to use as bookmarks or to put in a prominent place in their room at home.
- Instead of limiting the spiritual autobiography to the last activity, instruct the girls to begin the project in the first room and add to it in each successive room.
- Before each activity, explain the theme to one of the girls and ask her to choose a piece from *Listen for a Whisper: Prayers, Poems, and Reflections by Girls,* edited by Janet Claussen and Marilyn Kielbasa (Winona, MN: Saint Mary's Press, 2001). Use the piece to open or close the activity.

Scriptural Connections

Room 1
- Psalm 139 (God knew us before we were born.)
- Isa. 43:1 (God calls us by name.)

Room 2
- Mic. 6:8 (Act justly.)
- Matt. 5:1–16 (Treat others as God's children.)

Room 3
- Psalm 27 (My hope is in God.)
- Rom. 10:8–15 (Proclaim the Resurrection to all.)

Room 4
- Isa. 49:13–16 (God, like a mother, will not forget us.)
- Wisd. of Sol. 7:23—8:8 (These are the qualities of wisdom.)

Room 5
- Psalm 150 (Praise for God's greatness)
- Col. 3:12–17 (Duties of a Christian)

Room 6
- Matt. 7:7–11 (Ask God and seek God.)
- Luke 11:5–15 (Persevere in prayer.)

Room 7
- Ps. 25:1–10 (Pray for guidance and deliverance.)
- Ps. 62:1–2,5–8 (My soul rests in God.)

Background Information:
The Life and Spirituality of Teresa of Ávila

Teresa was born 28 March 1515, in Ávila, Spain, to Beatriz de Ahumada and Alonzo Sanchez de Cepeda. She was one of twelve children. Her father was a wealthy cloth merchant, having inherited his profession from his father, who was a Jewish Christian. Teresa said little about her childhood, but we know that her parents modeled both personal piety and social compassion.

Teresa's adolescence was spent absorbed in the typical concerns of that age-group. She desired a good social image and reputation. The cultural norms of honor both preserved and tempted her. When she was sixteen, her father sent her to Our Lady of Grace convent school. She became quite ill and had to leave. That period of illness gave her time to reflect on her religious beliefs and on her life. She decided to become a Carmelite, and entered the order against her father's wishes at age twenty.

Her life in the Carmelite monastery was uneasy. She feared imperfection in her prayer life and became upset over unimportant situations. As time passed, she realized that the way of life in the monastery made it difficult for anyone to find uninterrupted time for silence, prayer, and meditation.

Eventually, Teresa established her own Carmelite monastery, one where the sisters lived in strict enclosure, spending their days in work, prayer, and celebration. Several other houses followed.

Teresa was a prolific writer. Much of what we know about the establishment of convents comes from her letters and documentation. We know of her life through her autobiography, *The Book of Her Life*. It is a mix of recounted events and descriptions of prayer. She wrote another book on prayer for her Carmelite sisters, *The Way of Perfection*. Many years later, she wrote *The Interior Castle*, which deals with the subject of prayer in a more systematic fashion than do her earlier works, reflecting a more mature, peaceful spirit. *The Book of Her Foundations* provides an account of many incidents and events in Teresa's life, covering the beginnings of each new house and describing people who were dear to her.

The year 1582 was a wearying one of travel, conflict, and illness for Teresa. In September, she experienced a severe hemorrhage, and she never left her bed after that. She died on the evening of 4 October, the feast of Saint Francis of Assisi.

(This section is based on Rosemary Broughton, *Praying with Teresa of Ávila*, pp. 14–26.)

Notes

Use this space to jot ideas, reminders, and additional resources.

Part B

Phenomenal Female
Visionaries and Prophets

Sr. Thea Bowman

Overview

Thea Bowman—singer, dancer, liturgist, educator, and evangelist—spent her life preaching the Good News as an African American and a Franciscan sister. She was an exuberant woman who found the common thread that interweaves people of all races, colors, and creeds. She traveled throughout the United States, speaking to many groups and promoting cultural awareness.

Throughout a lifetime of ministry, Sister Thea used her gifts to bring hope to the despairing, consolation to the suffering, and light to those in darkness, and to challenge all. Sister Thea's life was a witness to the power of song and story and their capacity to teach, inspire, correct, challenge, and transform.

The activities in this chapter are appropriate for girls in both middle school and high school.

Thematic Activities

Woman of Song, Woman of Courage (40–55 minutes)

Preparation
○ Prepare to give the girls the background information on the mission and lifework of Sr. Thea Bowman from the end of this chapter.
○ Recruit a volunteer to read resource 2, "Sr. Thea Bowman, Woman of Song," in a fluid, storytelling style.
○ Bring in a recording of, or music for, an African American spiritual.

1. Introduce Sr. Thea Bowman by leading a discussion of questions and comments like these:
  ◉ Have you ever been so moved by a piece of music that it made you cry or lifted your spirits? If so, what was that piece?

@ Have you ever listened to a song and remembered exactly where you were, who you were with, and even what you were feeling when you heard it once before? If so, what was that song?

@ If the answer to either of those questions is yes, then you—like most human beings—have been touched by the power of music. Listen to the story of one woman's experience of music in her life.

Invite the volunteer you recruited before the activity to read resource 2.

2. Present the following ideas in your own words:

@ Studies have found that music can stimulate creativity, focus thinking, and encourage spiritual growth. Music inspires courage, instills pride, relieves stress, and speaks to every aspect of our existence.

@ Music is an integral part of the spiritual journey of African Americans, as expressed in their sacred songs, called spirituals. Each spiritual is in its own way a prayer of yearning or celebration, of praise, petition, or contemplation, a simple lifting of the heart, mind, voice, and life to God.

@ Most spirituals focus on the ideas of freedom, hope, and faith in God, who saves and delivers from pain and suffering.

@ Music was a focal point of Sr. Thea Bowman's life, work, and mission. Through song and story, Sister Thea communicated joy, freedom, cultural pride, and a love for God.

Share with the girls a brief overview of the mission and lifework of Sr. Thea Bowman.

3. Play or sing the African American sacred song you have selected.

Variation 1. Encourage the girls to bring in and share recordings of songs that touch them or that evoke powerful memories. Invite them to describe their connection to each song. They might also find out what songs are particularly powerful for their friends. Try to discover common themes or characteristics.

Variation 2. Suggest that some girls research the effects of music on the human psyche and present their findings to the group.

Variation 3. Invite a music therapist to talk with the group about her or his work.

The Power of Song (25–35 minutes)

Preparation
○ Bring in a recording of an African American sacred song, or invite a local gospel choir or your school or parish choir to come in and perform such a song. A good resource for music is *Lead Me, Guide Me: The African American Catholic Hymnal,* by GIA Publications (Chicago: GIA Publications, 1987).

1. Invite the girls to find a quiet place in the room, where they will not be distracted. Tell them that they will hear a song from the African American tradition. Tell them to concentrate on the words of the song and on the scriptural images that come to mind. Encourage them to engage their imagination, to see and to hear the reality of the song.

When everyone is settled, play the recording or cue the choir. You may want to go through the song twice, so that the girls can concentrate on the words.

2. Ask the girls to name aloud the words or phrases from the song that they liked or connected with. Record their responses on the board. As words and phrases are called out, the girls will discover how differently each person heard what was sung. By collecting and reading the responses, the girls can help one another find a deeper connection with the words of the song and with the story behind the song.

3. Lead a discussion of questions such as these:
◉ What does the song tell you about African American history?
◉ What other spirituals do you know? [You might provide one or two familiar examples, such as "Amazing Grace" and "Swing Low, Sweet Chariot."]
◉ What are common themes of the spirituals you are familiar with?
◉ What do you think we can learn from spirituals?

4. Give the girls time to think and write about the music they like to listen to. Encourage them to consider what that music passes on to the listener, in contrast to what spirituals pass on.

Singing the Scriptures (20–40 minutes)

1. Give each girl a Bible and divide everyone into groups of four to six people. Ask each group to find a biblical text that speaks of a particular theme, such as hope and healing, or joyful praise. You may want to assign a different theme to each group. Direct the groups each to discuss how that passage might relate to their own life and what message it conveys.

2. Announce that each group is to write a song that conveys the message of its passage. Explain that the groups can use a familiar tune and set to it parts of the scriptural text and its meaning, or they can compose a new melody.

3. Invite the groups to take turns presenting their completed songs. Then discuss with the girls how it felt to communicate sacred texts through music.

The Cypress Will Grow (35–40 minutes)

The 18-minute video *The Cypress Will Grow* traces the history of African Americans within the church. It is available from the United States Conference of Catholic Bishops, at *www.nccbuscc.org/publishing/multicultural/african.htm* or 800-235-8722.

After viewing the video, invite discussion and dialogue, using the following sentence-starters:

◉ The video taught me . . .

◉ I never knew . . .

◉ Something I still do not understand is . . .

◉ I would like to know about . . .

◉ What I appreciate most about the African American culture is . . .

Preaching the Word (20–30 minutes)

Our Baptism calls us to bring the good news of Jesus Christ to the world. "I don't preach, I just tell the story of how God has been to me," Sister Thea would say. This activity offers the girls an opportunity to celebrate the women in the church who are preaching the Good News.

Preparation

○ Provide note cards with envelopes, and postage stamps, one for each girl.

1. Read the following excerpt from one of Sister Thea's speeches:

◉ "When I was a little girl in Canton, Mississippi, I went to those old black churches, and I learned what they called the old-time religion. I wanted to grow up to be a preacher.

". . . I can preach in the streets. I can preach in the neighborhood. I can preach in the home. I can preach and teach in the family. And it's the preaching that's done in the home that brings life and meaning to the Word your priest proclaims in his official ministry in the pulpit. . . .

". . . We've come into the Lord's house in prayer and in community to honor the women. And when we honor the women, we honor you, too, men and children, because we honor your mothers and wives and lovers and sisters and daughters, aunts and nieces, and friends.

"I invite all of you to pause a moment and bring to mind the women who gave you life, who nurtured you, who gave you light and laughter and faith and love. Did those women preach, did they teach, did they testify, did they witness?" (Celestine Cepress, ed., *Sister Thea Bowman, Shooting Star*, pp. 76–77).

2. Invite the girls to reflect on the women in their own community who have preached the Good News to them, through their words and by their example. Offer the following questions for reflection. If the girls know one another well, consider inviting them to share their responses to a few of the questions.

◉ Who are the women who have taught you?

◉ Who are the women who speak out against injustice?

◉ Who are the women who lead you in prayer?

◉ Who are the women who have given you counsel and spiritual guidance?

◉ Who are the women who reflect God's presence in the world?

◉ What are a few characteristics of those women?

3. Create groups of four to six girls. Direct the girls each to choose one woman that they named in their reflection and to share with their group how that woman has lived out the call to preach the Good News and witness to the power of God in her life.

4. Distribute note cards, and invite the girls to write a short note of thanks and affirmation to the woman they talked about in their group. Supply envelopes and stamps, or collect the notes and send them for the girls.

Variation. Instead of having the girls write a note to a woman they have learned from, call them to reflect on the following question: "Who would name *you* as someone who preaches the Good News by words and actions?" Direct them to write a note to themselves telling how their life preaches the Good News. Suggest that if they cannot come up with concrete examples, they write about how they would like to preach the Good News, then use the note as a tool for personal growth.

Prayer Service (5–10 minutes)

Preparation
○ Provide music for an appropriate song in the African American tradition, such as "There Is a Balm in Gilead" (*Lead Me, Guide Me,* no. 157).

1. Sing a verse, or a verse and a refrain, from the song you have chosen.

2. Read the following excerpt:
◉ "Thea Bowman calls us to be children in love with the beauty and power of the creation of God. No one can be left out. No one can be defined to the back of the bus, the curb of the road. . . . No one can be thrown into the shadows of neglect and invisibility. 'There's plenty good room in the kingdom' and we must be about inviting all we meet to join us at the welcome table.

"We pray to you God, who has guided us with a mother's love and watched over us with a father's tender care. Help us to see clearly and remember truly the life and power of Sister Thea, a woman who held on to her faith, even when the 'storms of life' were raging. Like her, we ask you to 'stand by us.' We pray this in Jesus' name. Amen" (quoted and adapted from Joseph A. Brown, "Prayer Service Honoring Sr. Thea Bowman").

3. Sing another verse, or verse and refrain, of the song you began the prayer service with.

Options and Actions

• Celebrate Sister Thea's feast day on 30 March. Invite the girls to conduct a parish- or school-wide prayer service honoring Sister Thea.

- Ask the girls to profile African American women who have contributed to the church, the community, or society as a whole. Submit their written tributes to local newspapers or publish them in your parish bulletin or school newsletter. Publicly acknowledge those women at parish or school events or liturgies.

- November is Black Catholic History Month, a time to celebrate the long history and proud heritage of Black Catholics and of Catholicism. Contact your diocesan office for materials, or log on to *www.bcimall.org/bchmat01.htm,* hosted by the Catholic African World Network, 313-521-7777.

- African brooms, water, soil, black pots, plants, branches, quilts, cowbells, and other items are used as liturgical symbols to connect African American history to the present. Instruct the girls to find out the origins of such symbols and the reasons why they are used. *Vibrant Worship with Youth,* edited by Brian Singer-Towns (Winona, MN: Saint Mary's Press, 2000), discusses such symbols.

- Explore the history of the African American music culture. Contact the Smithsonian Institution at *www.si.edu/folkways/40076.htm* or 800-410-9815 to obtain four audiocassettes of music from the National Public Radio series *Wade in the Water: African American Sacred Music Traditions.*

- Help the girls make a story quilt. Invite them to write about an important event or factor that has made them who they are. Then have each girl transfer the image onto a fabric quilt block, using iron-on transfers or fabric crayons, markers, or paints. Recruit volunteers who have sewing skills to sew the blocks together, or invite adult quilters to teach the entire group how to sew the squares together.

- Attend an African American liturgy with the girls. Or help the girls arrange for a local gospel choir to share their music at a school or parish Mass.

- Explore the hymnal *Lead Me, Guide Me,* particularly its preface, which includes the article "The Gift of African American Sacred Song," by Sister Thea.

Scriptural Connections

- Gen. 1:26–27 (We are made in God's image.)
- Exod. 15:20–21 (Sing to the Lord.)
- Psalm 150 (Praise God in song.)
- 1 Cor. 12:12–31 (Live in unity.)

Resource Materials

Print

Bowman, Thea, ed. *Families: Black and Catholic, Catholic and Black.* Washington, DC: United States Conference of Catholic Bishops, 1985.

Brown, Joseph A. *A Retreat with Thea Bowman and Bede Abram: Leaning on the Lord.* Cincinnati: St. Anthony Messenger Press, 1997.

Cepress, Celestine, ed. *Sister Thea Bowman, Shooting Star: Selected Writings and Speeches.* La Crosse, WI: Franciscan Sisters of Perpetual Adoration, 1999.

Koontz, Christian, ed. *Thea Bowman: Handing On Her Legacy.* Kansas City, MO: Sheed and Ward, 1991.

Video

Balm in Gilead: The Legacy of African American Spirituals. KCNC-TV. 1997. 21 minutes. The station will provide a complimentary videocassette to any school or institution. Contact the KCNC-TV public affairs desk, 303-830-6555.

Old-Time Religion. Treehaus Communications. 1988.

Sister Thea: Her Own Story. Oblate Media and Communications. 1991. 93 minutes.

Internet

www.nccbuscc.org/saac/index.htm. Secretariat for African American Catholics. Visit the Web site or call 202-541-3177.

Background Information:
The Life and Spirituality of Sr. Thea Bowman

Sr. Thea (Bertha) Bowman was born 29 December 1937, in Yazoo City, Mississippi. She was the only child of Dr. Theon Edward Bowman and Mary Esther Bowman. She grew up in Canton, Mississippi, where her father had his medical practice, and she became a member of the Catholic church at the age of nine.

In September 1948, her parents enrolled her in the newly opened Holy Child Jesus School, staffed by the Franciscan Sisters of Perpetual Adoration from La Crosse, Wisconsin. In 1953, when she was fifteen, she decided to enter the community of sisters who had taught her. At her reception into the novitiate in 1956, she received the name Sister Thea.

Gifted with a brilliant mind, a beautiful voice, and a dynamic personality, Sister Thea shared the message of God's love through a teaching career. After she had taught for sixteen years at the elementary, secondary, and university levels, the bishop of Jackson, Mississippi, invited her to become the diocesan consultant for intercultural awareness. In that position, Sister Thea frequently worked with children to help them grow in awareness of their gifts and of their cultural heritage. Through song, dance, poetry, drama, and story, she communicated joy, freedom, and pride, using traditional Black teaching techniques that were holistic, participatory, and focused on reality. Music was one of her focal points.

Her programs were directed toward breaking down racial and cultural barriers. She encouraged people to communicate with one another so that they could understand other cultures and races. Sister Thea made more than one hundred public appearances each year, preaching, teaching, singing, and spreading the message that we are all worthy.

In 1984, Sister Thea was diagnosed with terminal bone cancer. She prayed, "I want to live as fully as I can live until I die" (Celestine Cepress, ed., *Sister Thea Bowman, Shooting Star,* p. 117). In 1989, the American bishops invited her to be a keynote speaker at their conference on Black Catholics. At the end of the meeting, at Sister Thea's invitation, the bishops stood and sang "We Shall Overcome."

In Nigeria, Kenya, Canada, the Virgin Islands, and Hawaii, from New York to Florida, Mississippi to California, and Louisiana to Illinois, thousands of people were touched by Sister Thea. She made people more aware of their own gifts and potential, and put races in touch with one another. Her ministry was a ministry of joy. Sister Thea died in 1990.

Notes

Use this space to jot ideas, reminders, and additional resources.

Sr. Thea Bowman, Woman of Song

When I was a child in Canton, Mississippi, my people sang the songs of faith—songs of Adam and Eve, Cain and Abel, Noah, Moses, David, and Jesus. The songs of faith were passed on, taught, learned, and prayed in an environment of love and celebration. I learned them from Mama, who sang me to sleep, who sang for me and with me in so many special and well-remembered moments; from Mother Rica who gathered twenty-five or thirty children around her in her warm home and sang faith songs that called forth energy and enthusiasm, that invited bodily response, that were fun; from Mrs. Ward, our next-door neighbor, who sang as she worked her garden or hung out wash and fed her chickens, who hummed as she walked down the street; from other children who sang as they played church and baptism and funeral, or as they sang for simple entertainment and joy; from Sayde and Earnest Garrett and the other Garrett brothers who gathered around our piano and sang with us for hours whenever they came to visit; from all the church folks who sang, played instruments, and danced, or who in their faces and bodies reflected the power and beauty of the songs of faith. Sharing the songs of faith bonded us in family and church. Sharing the songs brought hope and consolation and joy.

I did not realize I was receiving a religious education—that I was being taught prayer, salvation history, morals and values, faith, hope, love, and joy. (Thea Bowman, FSPA, *Sister Thea: Songs of My People, a Compilation of Favorite Spirituals* [Boston: St. Paul Books and Media, 1989], page 3. Copyright © 1988 by Daughters of Saint Paul. As quoted in *Sister Thea Bowman, Shooting Star: Selected Writings and Speeches,* edited by Celestine Cepress, FSPA [La Crosse, WI: Franciscan Sisters of Perpetual Adoration, 1999], pages 43–44. Copyright © 1999 by Franciscan Sisters of Perpetual Adoration. Used with permission of Pauline Books and Media, 50 Saint Paul's Avenue, Boston, MA 02130. All rights reserved.)

Sr. Helen Prejean

Overview

This chapter offers an opportunity for the girls to explore the life and mission of Sr. Helen Prejean, internationally known for her work to abolish capital punishment. Sister Helen's work shows how one voice can make a resounding difference in today's world. This chapter invites the girls to learn, to act, and to pray—three simple steps that changed the course of Sister Helen's life. The activities are most appropriate for girls in high school, though some adaptation could be made for a younger group.

Thematic Activities

A Mission for Life (40–55 minutes)

Preparation
○ Prepare to give the girls the background information on the mission and lifework of Sr. Helen Prejean from the end of this chapter.
○ Consider obtaining a copy of *Dead Man Walking: An Eyewitness Account of the Death Penalty in the United States*, by Helen Prejean (New York: Random House, 1993), for your own reference and enrichment. You might also view the film *Dead Man Walking* (PolyGram Filmed Entertainment, 1995, 122 minutes, rated R).

1. Provide a brief overview of the life and work of Sr. Helen Prejean. Explain that to fully appreciate Sister Helen and her ministry, the girls must learn more about the important work she has undertaken. Mention that this first activity allows the girls to discover what they already know about the debate surrounding capital punishment.

2. Announce that you will offer several statements that require some thought and dialogue. Ask the girls to line up in the center of the room. Designate one side of the room "Strongly agree" and the other side "Strongly disagree." Note that after you read each statement, the girls should move to the point in the room that best reflects their beliefs.

Read the following statements, pausing after each one to allow the girls to choose their position and to lead a brief discussion about who is standing where and why:

- ◉ I would visit someone who is in prison.
- ◉ Everyone in prison is guilty of some crime.
- ◉ When someone is convicted of a crime, where she or he lives influences the type of sentence.
- ◉ The death penalty is unfair.
- ◉ Capital punishment is a deterrent to murder.
- ◉ People who commit horrible crimes are not redeemable in the eyes of God.

3. Read resource 3, "Speaking Out Against the Death Penalty." Invite the girls to jot down words and images that describe Sister Helen as they listen to her words. Read the piece slowly and deliberately, pausing after each excerpt to allow the girls to process it.

4. Ask the girls to describe Sister Helen and her work by naming aloud some of the words and images that came to mind as they listened to her words. Continue the discussion, using questions like these:

- ◉ Is there anything extraordinary about this woman?
- ◉ Are you impressed by her? If so, what do you admire most about her?
- ◉ Why might members of the church applaud her efforts?
- ◉ Why might we as women applaud her efforts?

Variation 1. Use study materials from the Religious Organizing Against the Death Penalty Project (*www.deathpenaltyreligious.org* or 215-241-7130), and the video and book *Dead Man Walking* to prepare a more detailed presentation on Sister Helen's life and work. Or make those materials available to the girls and direct them to conduct the presentation.

Variation 2. Instead of reading resource 3, read all or part of Sister Helen's speech at an interreligious service to protest the death penalty in Albany, New York, on 24 January 1995. The script can be found at *www.bway.net/~halsall/radcath/prejean1.html*. In it, Sister Helen explains why she became involved in the death penalty issue and how the book and movie titled *Dead Man Walking* relate to her experiences.

Called to Learn (30–60 minutes)

1. Divide the girls into small groups and give each group newsprint and markers. Ask the groups each to list reasons they have heard for supporting the death penalty.

2. Call the groups to share their completed lists with everyone. Then lead a discussion focused around questions such as these:

- ◉ What do the Scriptures say about capital punishment?
- ◉ What is the Catholic church's stance on the death penalty?

- How could victims and their families obtain justice if the death penalty were not an option?
- How could victims and their families find some sense of closure if the death penalty were not an option?
- Are there other reasons for opposing the death penalty? If so, what are they?

Make the following points during the discussion or by way of summary:

- Following the life and teachings of Jesus leads to compassion and care for victims of crime. The church must stand in a special way with those who have experienced violence. Opposing the death penalty does not undermine that support, nor does it imply a willingness to let crime go unpunished.
- Justice can be achieved without more killing. Many victims' families affirm that closure comes through forgiveness and reconciliation, not more violence.
- Other reasons for opposing the death penalty include these:
  - Mistakes can and have been made. A number of prisoners on death row have been found innocent.
  - The death penalty is applied in a discriminatory way. People who are poor and members of minority groups are more likely to be sentenced to death.
  - Executions undermine our society by promoting hatred and revenge.
- Often, we hear a Bible passage quoted to justify capital punishment: "fracture for fracture, eye for eye, tooth for tooth" (Lev. 24:20). That follows a more direct passage: "Anyone who kills a human being shall be put to death" (v. 17). People who emphasize those passages ignore similar passages in which death is decreed for one who works on the Sabbath (Exod. 31:15) or for one who curses a parent (Exod. 21:17) or for a rebellious teenager (Deut. 21:18–21).
- Jesus rejected violence, oppression, and alienation. His life and teachings invite people into a new style of living: the Reign of God. Intimacy and trust, compassion and forgiveness, concern for justice, and nonviolence are key aspects of this new life.
- Since 1980, many individual bishops and state conferences of bishops have expressed their opposition to the death penalty, frequently appealing to the consistent ethic of life as the basis of their position. Four values express the heart of their position:
  - First, ending capital punishment is a way to break the cycle of violence. There are more humane and more effective responses to the growth of violent crime, including paying attention to the root causes such as poverty and injustice.
  - Second, abolishing the death penalty affirms the belief in the unique worth and dignity of every person.
  - Third, abolishing the death penalty expresses the fundamental belief that God is the ruler of life and that human beings are to exercise good steward-ship but not absolute control of life.
  - Fourth, ending the death penalty is consonant with the example of Jesus. The God revealed in the life of Jesus is a God of forgiveness and redemption, of love and compassion.

@ On Good Friday 1999, the United States Conference of Catholic Bishops remembered Jesus' execution with a bold call to all people of goodwill to work to end capital punishment. They said, "The death penalty offers the tragic illusion that we can defend life by taking life."

Listen and Learn from the Stories (20–30 minutes)

The Lamp of Hope Project, founded by Texas death row prisoners, tells the stories of dozen of prisoners who await execution. This activity gives the girls a chance to hear real stories of real people.

Preparation

○ Review the prisoners' writings from the Lamp of Hope Project at *www.lampofhope.org,* and print enough prisoners' stories so that you have one for every four or five girls. (These stories can also be obtained by contacting the project's executive director at *aspanhel@airmail.net.*)

Divide the girls into groups of four or five. Give the groups each a prisoner's story, and ask them to read it aloud and consider questions like the ones that follow:

@ Describe the person you read about.
@ How is he or she similar to you?
@ How is he or she different from you?
@ How do you think Sister Helen would respond if she met this person?
@ How do you think Jesus would respond to this person?
@ How would you respond if you met this person?

Prayer Service (10–15 minutes)

Preparation

○ Set up a simple prayer space with a crucifix, a candle, and a Bible. You may want to include items that highlight the work and mission of Sister Helen, such as a photo of her or a copy of the book or film *Dead Man Walking.* You also may want to include the names of people who have been executed in the past year; you can obtain a list of those names from the National Coalition to Abolish the Death Penalty, at *www.ncadp.org/html/factsandstats.html* or 202-387-3890.

○ Recruit a volunteer to read the words of Sister Helen from resource 4, "Prayer Service for Sr. Helen Prejean."

Gather the girls in the prayer space and invite the volunteer to join you in reading resource 4.

Variation. On separate pieces of paper, write the names of the prisoners who were executed in the past year, and distribute the papers equally among the girls. Have the girls read the names in turn, in litany fashion, and place them at the foot of the crucifix while the group responds, "God of justice, have mercy."

Options and Actions

Sister Helen's mission focuses on not only learning but also action, to move people to new understandings and appreciation of all human life. Her words cannot stand alone, nor can ours. Invite the group to choose one of the following ways to become more involved in Sister Helen's mission:

- Send a letter or a card of encouragement to someone who is awaiting execution. To obtain a list of names and addresses, contact the Death Row Support Project at *www.brethren.org/genbd/witness/DRSPbrochure.htm* or 219-982-7480, or use the list supplied by the Lamp of Hope Project at *www.lampofhope.org* or by the project's executive director at *aspanhel@airmail.net.* Caution the girls not to include their full name, a return address, or any other identifying information. Collect the letters and mail them yourself.

    Note: You may want to solicit parental permission before inviting the girls to participate in this activity. You also may want to invite the parents to review the letters with their daughters before they are sent.

- Send Sister Helen letters of affirmation or questions and comments. She is willing to receive correspondence at *hprejean@aol.com.*

- Write a moratorium statement. In 1997, the American Bar Association called for a moratorium on the death penalty until racial and income discrepancies could be studied. Since that time, a number of organizations have been urging faith groups and others to draft moratorium statements. The United States Conference of Catholic Bishops provides sample parish statements. Print the samples from *www.nccbuscc.org/sdwp/national/criminal/mortrm2k.htm* or call 202-541-3000.

- Sign a declaration of life. That is a document stating that if you are murdered, you do not want your perpetrator to be sentenced to death. For more information, print a sample from *www.webcom.com/peace/PEACTREE/fcl/edufund/dp-resource. html#insert2,* hosted by the Friends Committee on Legislation Education Fund, or call the fund at 916-443-3734. Make it clear that the declaration is simply a statement of intent, not a legally binding document.

    Note: You may want to solicit parental permission before inviting the girls to participate in this activity.

- Participate in International Death Penalty Abolition Day, on 1 March. This marks the day in 1847 when Michigan officially became the first English-speaking territory in the world to abolish capital punishment. It is a day to remember the victims of violent crimes and their survivors, to remember those killed by state-sanctioned violence, and to explore alternatives to the death penalty. For more information and an organizer's packet, contact Citizens United for Alternatives to the Death Penalty (CUADP) at *www.cuadp.org* or 800-973-6548.

- Plan and prepare an educational session for your parish, school, or community. Focus on speakers who can discuss the imprisonment of those who are innocent, developmentally disabled, and mentally ill. You might arrange for families of murder victims, death row survivors, and other knowledgeable speakers to visit your area. Contact CUADP at *cuadp@cuadp.org* or 800-973-6548.

- Participate in the Moratorium Now! campaign. The girls can initiate community involvement with this project, which includes a coordinated global petition drive. Contact the Quixote Center at *www.quixote.org/ej* or 301-699-0042.
- Begin a "toll campaign," asking local churches to ring their bells on the day of an execution. For more information, contact For Whom the Bells Toll at *www.curenational.org/~bells* or 781-391-9435.

Scriptural Connections

- Gen. 4:15 (Cain and Abel)
- Deut. 24:10–21 (miscellaneous laws)
- Matt. 5:43–48 (love for enemies)
- Matt. 7:1–5 (judging others)

Resource Materials

Print

Bedau, Hugo Adam, ed. *The Death Penalty in America: Current Controversies*. New York: Oxford University Press, 1997.

Megivern, James J. *The Death Penalty: An Historical and Theological Survey*. Mahwah, NJ: Paulist Press, 1997.

Video

Death No More: A Look at the Death Penalty. Brown-ROA Publishing. 1999. 40 minutes. Interview with Helen Prejean, hosted by David Haas.

Internet

www.amnesty-usa.org/abolish. Amnesty International. Visit the Web site or call 800-266-3789 or 212-807-8400.

www.deathpenaltyinfo.org. Death Penalty Information Center. The center provides curricula about the death penalty that are appropriate for high school students and young adults, and adaptable for parish use. Visit the Web site or call 202-293-6970.

www.cacp.org. Catholics Against Capital Punishment. Visit the Web site or fax the organization at 301-654-0925.

www.ncadp.org. National Coalition to Abolish the Death Penalty. Visit the Web site or call 202-387-3890.

Background Information:
The Life and Spirituality of Sr. Helen Prejean

Helen Prejean was born 21 April 1939, in Baton Rouge, Louisiana, and has lived and worked in Louisiana all her life. She was educated by the Sisters of Saint Joseph of Medaille, and joined the community in 1957.

Sister Helen's compassion for condemned people stems from her experience with poor people. A shabby house in New Orleans known as Hope House has been Sister Helen's home base, on and off, for over twenty years. She has lived with urban poverty, among drug sellers, gunfire, and deprived and abused children. Half of the young men in the area end up dead or in jail.

She began counseling her first death row inmate in 1982. Her grim register of pen pals is one element in a campaign that takes her to death row to visit inmates, to university campuses and dusty church halls to describe the horrors of the chair and lethal injection, and to Washington to battle her opponents in Congress. It also has won her international recognition.

Her passionate denunciation of the grisly process of putting someone to death, which she has witnessed herself, is both emotionally and rationally powerful. Undeniably persuasive though she is, she acknowledges that her crusade would never have gone far had it not been for the movie *Dead Man Walking*. The Oscar-winning film based on Sister Helen's book was a remarkable box office success. Directed by Tim Robbins and starring Susan Sarandon as Sister Helen, it tells the story of the nun's friendship with a man on death row. The prisoner in the movie is a composite of those Sister Helen had worked with over the years.

Conscious that her compassion for poor criminals could be misconstrued as a lack of compassion for victims, she has helped establish Survive, a victims' advocacy group. She has also befriended, prayed with, and supported many families of murder victims.

Sister Helen continues to counsel death row inmates and has accompanied five of them on their walk to death. She also continues her ministry to the families of murder victims. In a remarkably short time, Sr. Helen Prejean has become the most effective crusader against the death penalty in the United States.

Notes

Use this space to jot ideas, reminders, and additional resources.

Speaking Out Against the Death Penalty

The following excerpts are from Sister Helen's address at the Annual Public Gathering of the American Friends Service Committee on 6 November 1999. The entire address can be found at *www.afsc.org/crimjust/apgprejn.htm.*

> It took me . . . a long time to understand the connection between the Gospel message of Jesus Christ and justice. It has to be more than just being kind to individuals, but undoing the system that kills and hurts and maims people. Justice is a much harder thing to undertake than being charitable is.
>
> When I began to go, for the first time, into the soup kitchens and the places where homeless people were, there is something about being in the presence of people, real people who are suffering from injustice or racism that ignites our souls with a passion and we can't walk away from it.
>
> Energy comes to us because we get involved in something bigger than ourselves and our hearts have been moved by people's suffering, and we can't remain neutral. We say, "I don't know what I'm going to do but I've got to do something. I've got to get involved in some way."
>
> "Hey Sister Helen, you want to be a pen pal to somebody on death row?" I just said, "Sure, yeah. Give me their name." I thought that's all I was going to be doing.
>
> "Write a few letters." Sure, write a few letters, yeah. But then the person wrote back! I wasn't expecting all of this.
>
> The next thing I know I am accompanying this human being, Patrick Sonnier, walking with him with my hand on his shoulder. . . .
>   . . . I was walking with him and saying to him, "Patrick, when they do this thing, look at me. Look at my face."
>
> You cannot be there behind a Plexiglas screen and see the scripted death of a human being, being led into the room, strapped into a chair, a mask put over his face, and being killed in front of your eyes. You cannot be there and be in the presence of that kind of light, that kind of blinding light, and walk out and say, "I'm not going to do this any more."
>
> Something ignited in my own soul and I guess the basic thing was that I realized that I was a witness. I had seen the death penalty close up.
>
> And so my mission was born to begin to speak about the death penalty to anybody who would hear me.

Most of the pro-life people I met, they're pro innocent life, but they're sure not pro guilty life. Is there a difference? Was the Gospel of Jesus and who Jesus came to just the innocent, or is there a way that we can stand in the dignity of all human life, even those among us who have done terrible crimes?

The only way we can kill each other is when we're disconnected and we're allowed to say, "Oh, they're not human the way we're human and it's okay. They did this crime and it's okay to kill them."

If there is a part of you outraged over crimes, saying these people deserve to die, you've got to ask yourself an honest question: Are you willing to pull the switch?

The only way to change things is to change consciousness. The only way to change consciousness is by people dialoguing and talking to each other in little bits.

(As quoted at *www.afsc.org/crimjust/apgprejn.htm,* accessed 9 July 2001. Copyright © American Friends Service Committee. Used with permission.

Prayer Service
for Sr. Helen Prejean

Leader: Fears and gut-level reactions may cry out for vengeance, but Jesus' example in the Gospels invites us to develop a new and different attitude toward violence. So we need to pray, asking God for a change of heart. Old habits and prejudgments may be hard to remove.

We conclude this time together with the closing words that Sister Helen spoke in a speech in Albany, New York. We pray in solidarity with her, and we pray especially for all those who work diligently for justice.

Reader: *[Light a candle, then read the following excerpt:]* "Here in this place, with the beauty and richness of our faith—the beauty and richness of all the people here— we light a candle, a light in the midst of the darkness, to say that we are people of life and not death, a people of compassion and not vengeance.

"Let us carry on the work of lighting candles here and in the hearts of people everywhere to let them know how we feel about the death penalty and to work for its abolition" (adapted from a speech given by Helen Prejean, CSJ, at an interreligious service to protest the death penalty, in Albany, New York, on 24 January 1995, as quoted at *www.bway.net/~halsall/radcath/prejean1.html,* accessed 9 July 2001; copyright © American Friends Service Committee).

Leader: We pray, God, that you will bless us, and go before us in the flame of this candle, that we may carry in our hearts a reminder of our desire to be cocreators of peace and justice in our world. Amen.

Dorothy Day

Overview

The Catholic Worker movement began simply enough on 1 May 1933, when journalist Dorothy Day and philosopher Peter Maurin teamed up to publish and distribute the *Catholic Worker,* a newspaper promoting the biblical promise of justice and mercy. The movement was committed to nonviolence, voluntary poverty, and practicing the works of mercy as a way of life. Dorothy and Peter opened a "house of hospitality," where people who were homeless, hungry, and forsaken would always be welcome. (Adapted from "The Catholic Worker Movement Described in 120 Words")

The activities in this chapter introduce a woman whose radical commitment to the Gospel, whose commitment to the Catholic church, and whose willingness to live her beliefs led her to make a profound difference in the world. All the activities are appropriate for high school girls; many can also be used with younger teens.

Thematic Activities

Discovering Dorothy Day (40–55 minutes)

Preparation
- Obtain self-stick notes in three colors, five or six of each color for each girl, plus extras.
- Post three sheets of newsprint and title them, "I know," "I want to know," and "I learned." List the following topics down the left side of each sheet:
  - Life
  - Work
  - Faith life and religious practice
  - Political views
  - Legacy

○ Arrange for the girls to have access to the Internet, or make available several resources on the life and work of Dorothy Day. Some useful Web sites and reading materials are listed in the resource materials section near the end of this chapter.

○ Prepare to give the girls the background information on the mission and lifework of Dorothy Day from the end of this chapter. You may also want to read *The Long Loneliness: The Autobiography of Dorothy Day* (San Francisco: HarperSanFrancisco, 1997; also available from other publishers).

1. Ask the girls if they are familiar with the Catholic Worker movement and its founders, Peter Maurin and Dorothy Day. Explain that they will spend some time learning about a radical woman who started a radical movement because of her belief in Gospel values and in the dignity of every person.

2. Distribute five or six self-stick notes of one color to each girl. Point out the sheet of newsprint titled "I know." Instruct the girls to write a fact they know about Dorothy Day on each note and attach it to the newsprint under the appropriate topic. For example, they might write, "Started the Catholic Worker movement," and post it under the topic "Work." Some people may not use all their notes; others may need extras.

After everyone has posted their notes, review with the group all the facts listed on the newsprint.

3. Distribute five or six notes of a second color to each girl. Point out the newsprint headed "I want to know." Tell the girls to write on each note something they would like to know about Dorothy Day. When everyone has posted their notes under the proper heading, review the things people want to know.

4. Divide the girls into five groups. Assign each group one topic from the "I want to know" list and give it the notes under that section. Also give each group five or six notes of a third color. Tell the groups they have 20 minutes to use the resources you have supplied (the Internet, or books and articles) to find the information requested by the group, and as many related facts as possible. Direct them to write the facts on the blank notes and post them on the newsprint headed "I learned."

5. Present a brief biography of Dorothy Day, using the material you prepared before the activity and the notes the girls posted in steps 2 to 4.

6. Make the following comments in your own words:
◉ Dorothy Day made a tremendous impact on America, simply by living out her belief that every person, no matter what the circumstances, has a God-given right to a life of dignity. Her message, rooted in the Gospel, was not comfortable for many people. However, like Jesus, Dorothy Day devoted her life to comforting the disturbed and disturbing the comfortable.

Variation. If you think the girls are not familiar enough with Dorothy Day or her work, omit steps 2 to 4 of this activity. Make and post just one newsprint sheet, with the title "About Dorothy Day" and the five headings down its left side.

Divide the girls into five groups and assign each group one of the topics listed on the newsprint. Direct the groups to use the Internet, or books and articles supplied by you, to find out as much as they can about their topic in 20 minutes. Instruct them to write all their facts on the newsprint, under the appropriate heading. Conclude with a brief biography of Dorothy, incorporating the girls' facts and the comments listed in step 6 of the activity description.

"A Permanent Revolution" (150–180 minutes)

This activity involves watching the film *Entertaining Angels,* a biography of Dorothy Day. Allow enough time for viewing and discussion, if necessary covering the movie in parts over two or more days.

Preparation

○ Obtain the film *Entertaining Angels: The Dorothy Day Story* (Paulist Pictures, 1996, 112 minutes, rated PG-13). Preview the film, noting particular scenes, ideas, and dialogue that you want to discuss with the girls.

1. Recruit a volunteer, give her a Bible, and ask her to read Heb. 13:1–2,5–6 aloud. Discuss the meaning of the passage, focusing on the notion of entertaining angels without knowing it—that is, of extending authentic hospitality to everyone, not just those we consider worthy of it.

2. Explain to the girls that they will be seeing a movie about a woman for whom hospitality meant not simply being nice to strangers but leading a permanent and radical revolution grounded in the Gospel. View the movie with the girls.

3. Lead a discussion, using questions like these as a guide:
◉ Did anything surprise you about Dorothy Day's life? If so, what?
◉ What talents and abilities did she possess? Was she extraordinary in any way?
◉ What did the word *hospitality* mean to her?
◉ What did she mean by "a permanent revolution"?
◉ How did becoming a Catholic affect her life?
◉ How did being a woman affect her spirituality?
◉ How did being a woman affect her work?

4. Read the Beatitudes from Matt. 5:3–11. Invite the girls to offer spontaneous prayers in Dorothy's name for those touched by her life and work.

Variation. As part of the discussion of the movie, review the corporal and spiritual works of mercy. Ask the girls to list the works of mercy that Dorothy Day addressed. Note that both Dorothy Day and Peter Maurin were committed to practicing the works of mercy in their life and work.

A Saint Is . . . (20–30 minutes)

Preparation

○ Post several sheets of newsprint on a wall, to create a graffiti board. Write along the top of the newsprint, "A saint is . . ." Provide markers.

○ Create prayer cards from resource 5, "'Prayer for the Canonization of Servant of God Dorothy Day,'" one card for each girl.

1. Direct the girls' attention to the sheets of newsprint and the heading "A saint is . . ." Ask three or four volunteers to complete the sentence, and write their answers on the newsprint.

2. Encourage the girls to name some things about Dorothy Day's early life that many people would consider unsaintly. They may offer examples such as her support for communist and Marxist ideas, her denial of God and organized religion, her relationships with men, her common-law marriage, and her abortion.

Discuss how some parts of Dorothy's early life are not in keeping with traditional definitions of a saint as a pious, selfless, pure, and blameless person. Also point out that many Catholics are hoping for and working toward her canonization.

Then lead a discussion of questions like these:

◉ What qualifications does Dorothy have for sainthood?

◉ If you were in charge, would you make Dorothy a saint? Why or why not?

3. Divide the girls into pairs or small groups and distribute markers. Tell the pairs or groups to come up with a definition of a saint that includes people like Dorothy Day and to write it on the newsprint. You might offer quotes like the ones that follow, to get the girls thinking:

◉ "A saint is someone who makes it easier for others to believe in God."

◉ "A saint is a sinner who keeps on trying."

4. Review the new definitions with the group. Then make the following comments in your own words:

◉ Every person has the potential for sainthood, providing she or he lives as a witness to the Gospel message.

◉ In their search for God and for meaning in life, people make mistakes. Dorothy Day certainly did. When she was a young adult, some of her philosophies and moral choices were clearly not based on Gospel values. She was searching, and many times stumbled into the wrong place, with her priorities askew.

◉ However, when she recognized God's presence in her life and in the world, she accepted God's forgiveness and grounded the rest of her life in the Gospel. Her conversion to the Gospel and her willingness to live as a true disciple of Jesus'—no matter the cost—is what some say qualifies her for sainthood.

5. Distribute the prayer cards you created from resource 5 and say the prayer together. Encourage the girls to put their card where they will see it every day, and to continue to pray for the canonization of Dorothy Day.

Variation 1. Invite the girls to work together in pairs to create lines for a litany honoring Dorothy Day. For example, one line might be "Dorothy Day, friend of the poor" and another might be "Dorothy Day, challenger of social systems." Before the prayer for canonization, invite each pair to recite its line, followed by the group response, "Pray for us."

Variation 2. If the girls are not familiar with the lengthy process of official canonization in the church, lead them through its steps and requirements. Check your diocesan resource center for information, or log on to *saints.catholic.org/faq.html#choose,* hosted by Catholic Online.

The Magnificent Seven: Catholic Social Teaching (50–60 minutes)

This activity summarizes key principles and major themes of Catholic social teaching. As presented, it is best suited for younger teens. You can expand the exercise for older teens by incorporating more information from the *Catechism of the Catholic Church,* second edition, by the Libreria Editrice Vaticana (Washington, DC: United States Conference of Catholic Bishops [USCCB], 1997), part 3, chapters 1 and 2, particularly numbers 1877 to 1948. Also look at the document *Sharing Catholic Social Teaching: Challenges and Directions,* by the United States Conference of Catholic Bishops (Washington, DC: USCCB, 1998).

Preparation
○ Copy resource 6, "Seven Lessons for Our Time," and cut it apart as scored.
○ Gather seven sheets of poster board and a variety of used magazines, glue sticks, scissors, and markers.

1. Make the following comments in your own words:
◉ The life and work of Dorothy Day in many ways embodied the social teaching of the Catholic church. In fact, Dorothy advocated the strong statement on peace that emerged from Vatican Council II as the *Pastoral Constitution on the Church in the Modern World* (*Gaudium et Spes,* 1965). The church has adopted seven principles of justice to focus its work in that area.

2. Divide the young people into seven groups. Announce that each group will be given one of the seven principles of justice. The groups are to illustrate their principle with words and pictures, and show how it contradicts unjust practices of our time.

Give each group one principle from resource 6, a sheet of poster board, and used magazines, glue sticks, scissors, and markers. Suggest that the groups read and discuss their assigned principle and its accompanying world practices, and then create a poster illustrating both what the church teaches and how the world contradicts that teaching. Tell them to begin by writing the church principle on the poster in large, bold letters.

3. When the posters are finished, invite the groups to present them. Display the posters for all to see. Refer to them anytime you discuss justice issues with your group.

4. Ask the group which principles of justice Dorothy Day most closely aligned herself with, and what about her life or work supported each principle.

5. Close the activity with the prayer for Dorothy from resource 5.

(This activity is adapted from Joseph Grant, *Justice and Service Ideas for Ministry with Young Teens,* pp. 91–93.)

Variation. For the closing prayer, have each small group write a short petition based on its assigned principle. Set up a prayer space with seven candles, a Bible, and a crucifix. Ask a volunteer from each group to read the prayer while another volunteer lights one of the seven candles. After each prayer, lead the group in responding, "God of justice, hear our prayer." Close by reading Luke 4:18–19.

Prayer: A Decade with Dorothy Day (15–25 minutes)

Preparation
○ Ask the girls each to bring in a rosary, or provide one for each girl.
○ Create a simple prayer space with a Bible, a candle, and a crucifix. If you are providing rosaries, add them to the space.
○ Copy resource 7, "A Decade with Dorothy Day," and cut it apart as scored.

1. Gather the girls in a circle around the prayer space. Comment on Dorothy Day's great devotion to the suffering Jesus, as evidenced in her work with people who suffered. Convey the following information in your own words:
  ◎ Dorothy Day was a staunchly conservative Catholic who was devoted to magisterial authority and disliked many of the changes in the church brought about as a result of Vatican Council II. She favored traditional forms of prayer, once writing, "Every Catholic faced with a great need starts a novena" (*The Long Loneliness,* p. 283). One of her favorite forms of prayer was the rosary. This prayer activity combines that form with Dorothy's own words.
If the girls are not familiar with the rosary, explain it to them. Mention that a rosary typically contains five decades, but they will be praying only one in this activity.

2. Recruit ten readers and give each of them one of the readings from resource 7. Light the candle, then lead the girls in the sign of the cross and the Lord's Prayer. Invite the volunteer to do the first reading. After a few moments for reflection, lead the girls in reciting the Hail Mary. Follow the same process with all ten readings. Close with a recitation of the Glory Be, as you would every decade of the rosary.

Variation 1. Help the girls make their own rosary bracelets. Provide jute, leather cord, or elastic, and colored beads. Tell them to string ten beads, each signifying one Hail Mary, tying a knot after each to keep it in place.

Variation 2. Divide the girls into five groups. Provide each group with books and other resources by and about Dorothy Day. Instruct the groups each to find ten short readings, creating a decade of the rosary similar to the one in resource 7. You may want to assign a different theme to each group so that each decade is unique. Pray one decade a day, led by the group that found the readings.

Variation 3. "Decades of Mystery, Circle of Joy" is a full rosary prayer based on the global experiences of women and girls, written in a style similar to that of the rosary prayer in this activity. It can be found on pages 118–125 of *Prayer: Celebrating and Reflecting with Girls,* by Marilyn Kielbasa, another book in the Voices series.

Options and Actions

- If there is a Catholic Worker house of hospitality in your area, explore volunteer opportunities with and for the girls.
- Invite someone involved in the Catholic Worker movement to speak about Dorothy Day, her work, and her legacy. If there is no Catholic Worker group in your area, contact your diocesan office of social justice for speaker recommendations.
- Hold a community banquet in honor of Dorothy Day, who wrote, "Heaven is a banquet and life is a banquet, too, even with a crust, where there is companionship" (*The Long Loneliness,* p. 285). Do this at an established soup kitchen, for its regular guests, or as a parish fund-raiser for the local Catholic Worker community.
- If you work with older girls, encourage them to read and discuss *The Long Loneliness,* one chapter at a time.
- Dorothy Day was a founding member of Pax Christi USA, which is a national Catholic peace movement. Explore the history and the work of this organization at *www.paxchristiusa.org,* or by requesting information from Pax Christi USA, 532 West Eighth Street, Erie, PA 16502-1343, 814-453-4955 (phone), 814-452-4784 (fax).

Scriptural Connections

- Lev. 25:35–38 (Look after the poor as you do a stranger.)
- Isa. 58:6–8 (Share bread, provide shelter.)
- Matt. 5:3–14 (The Sermon on the Mount)
- Rom. 12:6–13 (The marks of a true Christian)
- James 2:14–18 (Faith must be accompanied by good deeds.)

Resource Materials

Print

Allaire, James, and Rosemary Broughton. *Praying with Dorothy Day.* Winona, MN: Saint Mary's Press, 1995.

Coles, Robert. *Dorothy Day: A Radical Devotion.* Reading, MA: Addison-Wesley Publishing Co., 1987.

Quigley, Margaret, and Michael Garvey, eds. *The Dorothy Day Book.* Springfield, IL: Templegate Publishers, 1982.

Internet

www.catholicworker.org/index.cfm. Catholic Worker movement.

www.catholicworker.org/dorothyday/index.cfm. Catholic Worker movement, Dorothy Day Library.

www.justpeace.org/frontpage.htm. Justpeace. Robert Waldrop, 1524 NW Twenty-first Street, Oklahoma City, OK 73106.

www.paxchristiusa.org. Pax Christi USA, national Catholic peace movement. 814-453-4955.

Background Information:
The Life and Spirituality of Dorothy Day

Dorothy Day was born 8 November 1897 in Brooklyn, New York. Her father was a journalist, and his work required that the family move several times during Dorothy's childhood. The Days eventually returned to New York, where Dorothy became a journalist, following in the footsteps of her father.

Dorothy considered herself to be a political radical and experimented with socialism, Marxism, and anarchism. She marched with the suffragists for women's rights. Always standing on the side of the workers, the poor, and the disenfranchised, Dorothy was arrested more than once as a result of her protests and controversial articles. Some of her most moving writing was done in jail.

Throughout her early years, Dorothy struggled with issues of faith, God, and religion. While something inside made her want to believe, her association with the socialists and the Marxists caused her to reject faith and religion as crutches for people who were weak. Besides, she did not see organized religion standing up to change the system of injustice in the world, and that angered her.

Things changed for Dorothy when she met the love of her life, Forster Batting-ham, a biologist whose political views Dorothy shared. They lived in a common-law marriage, and Dorothy became pregnant. Forster did not believe in bringing children into the world. Dorothy had had an abortion earlier, when she feared that another man she loved would leave her, and that man had deserted her anyway. This time, she chose to have the baby. She also decided to have the baby baptized in the Catholic church, to give her child something she believed was lacking in her own life. Forster had said he would have nothing to do with her or the baby if they became Catholic, and he left.

Dorothy became more and more involved in the church and in the plight of the poor. She eventually met Peter Maurin, who helped deepen her appreciation of Catholicism, especially its social teaching. The two began a paper called the *Catholic Worker* to express the vision they shared. The first issue was published 1 May 1933, in the middle of the Great Depression.

The *Catholic Worker* succeeded immediately. Soon, volunteers arrived and built a community to feed homeless and unemployed people in the area. The first house of hospitality opened, and a movement was begun. Within a few years, thirty-three Catholic Worker houses and farms dotted the country. Today, there are over 130 Catholic Worker communities in the United States.

Over many decades, the Catholic Worker movement has protested injustice, war, and violence of all forms. Dorothy actively protested World War II and the Vietnam War. She supported conscientious objection as the only Christian response to war. She was jailed for her actions many times. In 1973, she picketed the Teamsters Union in support of Cesar Chavez and migrant workers in California's San Joaquin Valley, an action that resulted in her last jail sentence. Dorothy died 29 November 1980.

Notes

Use this space to jot ideas, reminders, and additional resources.

"Prayer for the Canonization of Servant of God Dorothy Day"

Prayer for
the Canonization of Servant of God
Dorothy Day

Merciful God, you called your servant
Dorothy Day to show us the face of
Jesus in the poor and forsaken.
By constant practice
of the works of mercy,
she embraced poverty and witnessed
steadfastly to justice and peace.
Count her among your saints
and lead us all to
become friends of
the poor ones of the earth,
and to recognize you in them.
We ask this through your Son.
Jesus Christ, bringer of good news
to the poor. Amen.

Prayer for
the Canonization of Servant of God
Dorothy Day

Merciful God, you called your servant
Dorothy Day to show us the face of
Jesus in the poor and forsaken.
By constant practice
of the works of mercy,
she embraced poverty and witnessed
steadfastly to justice and peace.
Count her among your saints
and lead us all to
become friends of
the poor ones of the earth,
and to recognize you in them.
We ask this through your Son.
Jesus Christ, bringer of good news
to the poor. Amen.

(This prayer is from Claretian Publications, 205 West Monroe Street, Chicago, IL 60606, 312-236-7782, extension 474, editors@uscatholic.org, as quoted at www.catholicworker.org/dorothyday/index.cfm, accessed 16 July 2001. Used with permission.

Seven Lessons for Our Time

Lesson 1

Catholic church principle. Life is sacred, and the dignity of the human person is to be respected.

World practices. capital punishment, legalized abortion, materialism, pornography, unrestrained commercialism and consumerism, drug trafficking and abuse

Lesson 2

Catholic church principle. All people are equal and have the right to participate fully in the life of their community.

World practices. individualism; class divisions and stereotyping; gender discrimination; ethnic, racial, and religious intolerance; neglect of immigrants and refugees

Lesson 3

Catholic church principle. All people are to be afforded human rights and challenged to live up to human responsibilities.

World practices. institutionalized racism, sexism, and ageism; neglect of minority communities; ethnic genocide; imprisonment of political dissidents; abuse of prisoners; denial of political and social freedoms

Lesson 4

Catholic church principle. We are called to emulate God by showing a special preference for those who are poor and weak.

World practices. neglect of those who are poor, those who are older, women and children; lack of affordable housing and medical care for those who are needy; a growing gap between impoverished and wealthy people and nations

Lesson 5

Catholic church principle. We work to continue God's plan for the earth. Work is dignified when workers' rights are protected and the economy serves the needs of all people.

World practices. displacement of people from their land, widespread unemployment and underemployment, unjust labor practices, low wages in impoverished countries, sweatshops, child labor, global systems of economic injustice

Reading 6

Catholic church principle. We belong to a global family and are challenged to promote peace and solidarity.

World practices. nationalism and economic competition, ethnic division, persecution of minority populations, small- and large-scale conflicts, gang violence

Lesson 7

Catholic church principle. We share one planet; we are stewards of God's garden earth.

World practices. environmental destruction, loss of habitat for creatures and people, unsustainable consumption of global resources

A Decade with Dorothy Day

Reading 1

We cannot love God unless we love each other, and to love we must know each other. We know [God] in the breaking of bread, and we know each other in the breaking of bread, and we are not alone any more.

Reading 2

I am praying because I am happy, not because I am unhappy. I did not turn to God in unhappiness, in grief, in despair—to get consolation, to get something from [God]. . . .

    . . . I [pray] because I want to thank [God].

Reading 3

The surest way to find God, to find the good, was through one's brothers [and sisters].

Reading 4

Once [the] sense of fear of the unknown was overcome . . . love would evoke . . . love, and mutual love would overcome fear and hatred.

Reading 5

Every one of us who was attracted to the poor had a sense of guilt, of responsibility. . . . We felt a respect for the poor and destitute as those nearest to God, as those chosen by Christ for His compassion.

Reading 6

If we are rushed for time, sow time and we will reap time. Go to church and spend a quiet hour in prayer. You will have more time than ever and your work will get done.

Reading 7

A deep abiding joy can only be ours if we emphasize the "primacy of the spiritual." . . . We must grow in faith, in our spiritual capacity to "do all things in [God] Who strengthens us."

Reading 8

Every good impulse, every noble deed we perform is of God, Christ in us. At the very same time there is an evil, complacent nagging going on, trying to discourage us. . . . If we have faith and hope it is impossible to be discouraged.

Reading 9

To convert the poor you must be like them; to convert the rich you must be unlike them.

Reading 10

We have all known the long loneliness and we have learned that the only solution is love and that love comes with community.

It all happened while we sat there talking, and it is still going on.

Women Martyrs in El Salvador

Overview

In the 1970s and 1980s, it fell to a tiny, impoverished country to represent most dramatically the ongoing Crucifixion of Jesus Christ in his people. Poor people in El Salvador have often suffered under the weight of an oppressive government. But in the 1970s, an awakened church joined the struggle for justice.

The women in this chapter immersed themselves in the world of the poor people of that country. The lives of Sr. Silvia Maribel Arriola, Sr. Maura Clarke, Jean Donovan, Sr. Ita Ford, Sr. Dorothy Kazel, and Laura López tell the story of El Salvador's struggle for justice and of the many women who walked the journey to freedom with its people. The activities in this chapter are most appropriate for girls in high school.

Thematic Activities

Six Women, One Shared Fate (40–55 minutes)

Preparation
○ Prepare to give the girls the background information on the civil war in El Salvador and on the mission and lifework of Sr. Silvia Maribel Arriola, Sr. Maura Clarke, Jean Donovan, Sr. Ita Ford, Sr. Dorothy Kazel, and Laura López, from the end of this chapter.
○ Consider bringing in a map or a globe to help you convey the background information.

1. Pose questions like the ones that follow and lead a discussion focused around them:

☞ What is a martyr?

☞ When you hear the word *martyr,* what images or ideas come to mind?

2. Present the following comments in your own words:

- ◈ Many of us think that persecution and martyrdom are things of the past. But they are going on all the time, and holy men and women all over the world are paying the ultimate price to keep faith and Gospel values alive.

Briefly describe the civil war in El Salvador and tell the stories of Sister Silvia, Sister Maura, Jean, Sister Ita, Sister Dorothy, and Laura. You may want to point out locations on a map or a globe as you are talking. Then present the following information in your own words:

- ◈ From the earliest days of the church, martyrs have been acknowledged as the image of Jesus Christ. Their lives reflect Jesus' compassionate, liberating life in the world.

- ◈ There are some differences between the six women whose stories I just told, and martyrs of the previous centuries. One obvious difference is that in El Salvador, the killers dared to call themselves Christian.

- ◈ In that overwhelmingly Catholic country, people were not killed simply for clinging to the faith or defending the church or proclaiming the name of Jesus, as Christians had been in earlier centuries. They died because they united with the oppressed and opposed injustice.

- ◈ The stories of those brave women and men, almost all of whom peacefully accepted their death, forgiving their persecutors, need to be told because those people show us what it means to lead an authentic Christian life.

- ◈ Like Jesus, the six women died because their faith had made them threatening to the power structures of their society. The martyrs of El Salvador are just a few among thousands of men and women who have given their life because of deeply held convictions and the willingness to stand up for them.

3. Tell the girls to move to a place in the room where they can be alone with their thoughts. Ask them to reflect on the following questions.

- ◈ Who are the most important people in your life?
- ◈ What are the most important beliefs or values in your life?

Invite the girls to share their responses with another person or with the entire group.

4. Divide the girls into small groups and give each group newsprint and markers. Explain that all people are entitled to some basic rights. Noting the stories of the six martyrs of El Salvador and the issues they worked and died for, invite each group to create its own declaration of rights. The declaration should include the things that the girls believe are essential for a happy and healthy life for human beings, who are created in the image of God.

5. Invite each group to share its completed list with the others. Post the lists and compare them to catch anything that is missing. Be sure that the concepts respect, freedom, equality, and dignity are represented or discussed.

Variation 1. If the girls are not familiar with martyrdom in the early church, review some of the history with them. Focus on saints the girls are familiar with, such as Stephen and Peter. If any churches in your area are named after martyrs, you may want to explore the stories of those people.

Variation 2. Instead of telling the stories of the martyred women yourself, select six girls to do so or assign one woman to each of six groups. Make the background information available, and encourage the girls to be creative. Provide props and simple costumes, or direct the girls to do so.

Variation 3. After the lists of rights are completed, suggest that the girls compare them with the U.S. Constitution and the U.S. Bill of Rights.

Variation 4. Pair the girls with someone from their group, and instruct the partners to call each other to be accountable for carrying out the group's declaration of rights. Have them meet periodically to check in with each other.

A Pledge for Justice and Peace (20–30 minutes)

1. Distribute handout 7, "A Pledge for Justice and Peace." Invite the girls to spend some quiet time writing their own pledge for justice and peace. Mention that each pledge should draw on the justice themes of the church. Explain that the pledge is a way to encourage the girls to commit themselves to working for charity, justice, and peace as disciples of Jesus Christ's.

2. Invite each girl to share her completed pledge aloud. You might also post the pledges on a parish or school bulletin board, or publish them in a bulletin or newsletter.

3. Discuss action steps for carrying out each pledge. For example, if a participant pledges to learn more about El Salvador, identify what she needs to do to accomplish that task. Suggest that everyone take at least one step toward their goal in the coming week.

Let's Get Political (15–20 minutes)

Lead the girls in a brainstorming session about ways they might become stronger advocates for justice and peace. Encourage the girls to be creative. Here are a few suggestions to get them thinking:
- Buy selectively! Organize a boycott of companies or products that violate your principles, and write the companies to tell them what changes you think they should make. Buy what you need from companies that are socially responsible. Generally, purchase third-world products only from co-ops, small farms, or small, family-owned businesses. Especially avoid plantation crops like coffee, cocoa, and bananas, which displace food production for local people.
- Write a song to organize and inspire people.

- Learn about unions. Get a union member to explain their purpose, history, and status. Unions are where many important political battles are fought and won.
- Learn another language. This will expand your political and cultural horizons in unexpected ways.
- Call a radio talk show and talk sensibly about a current political topic.
- Join or begin a study circle focusing on an issue you care about, and start reading, thinking, and talking about that issue.
- Adopt a politician. For example, write a monthly letter to your U.S. representative, senator, or president, or invite a school board member to lunch.
- Write to foreign governments with poor human rights records. Let them know that you care about what they do, and hold them to the same standards of human decency as you hold your own government. Contact Amnesty International at *www.amnesty.org,* 800-266-3789, or 212-807-8400 to find out about human rights records in various parts of the world.

Letters to the Editor (20–30 minutes)

Writing a letter to the editor is a wonderfully effective way for the girls to reach thousands of people about almost any justice issue. Equally important, politicians keep a close watch on letters to the editor, to monitor public opinion, and that directly affects the actions our government takes.

Preparation
○ Consider providing an assortment of current news magazines or newspapers.
○ Compile a list of local and national newspapers and magazines, and their postal addresses. If your group has access to the Internet, also provide e-mail addresses for newspapers and magazines that accept electronic letters to the editor.
○ Provide stationery, envelopes, and stamps.

1. Form groups of four to six girls, and invite the groups each to discuss a current news story with a justice theme. You may want to provide a selection of current news magazines or newspapers. Here are a few questions the girls might consider:
- What is the issue?
- Who is affected by the issue?
- How does the issue affect you?
- What do the Scriptures or church teachings say about the issue?
- Why is it important for people to speak out about the issue?

2. Tell the girls to share their viewpoint about this issue with thousands of people by writing a letter to the editor of a newspaper or magazine. Supply postal and e-mail addresses of local and national newspapers and magazines, and make stationery, envelopes, and stamps available. Provide the following guidelines to help ensure that the girls' letters will be considered for publication:
- Keep it short.
- Show that you care about and believe in what you are writing. If you are moved or angry, get that on paper.

- Have a clear point and make it. Ask someone else to read your letter to check you on this one.
- Include an interesting fact or argument.
- Write legibly, and include your name, address, and phone number to enable the editors to verify your letter.
- Send your letter to "Letters to the Editor" at the newspaper's or magazine's address.
- If you can get others to write to the same newspaper or magazine on the same subject, especially over a period of time and in increasing numbers, the editors may decide that your issue is worth attention.

3. Allow the groups to read their completed letters aloud or to exchange them and edit one another's. Encourage the girls to send their letters.

Prayer Service: Go Out and Be Light (15–20 minutes)

Preparation
- Set up a prayer table with six pillar candles at the center. In a basket at the foot of the table, place a small candle (such as a votive candle) for each girl.
- Consider using music throughout the prayer service, and a gathering and closing song on the theme justice, light, or discipleship.
- Recruit three readers for the prayer.

Gather the girls around the prayer table and distribute handout 8, "Go Out and Be Light." Lead the girls through the prayer service as it is outlined on the handout.

Variation. Place twelve additional candles around the room. Call a girl to light a candle as each suffering of the El Salvadorans is identified.

Options and Actions

- Outline the elements of political advocacy and the electoral process, including electing representatives who are sympathetic to human rights interests. Contact Project Vote Smart at *www.vote-smart.org* or 888-868-3762, for information on elected officials at various levels of government as well as information to help the girls track what is going on in Congress.
- Participate in Witness for Peace's Call-a-Week campaign to oppose the United States' policies of military and economic violence toward Latin America and to support policies for human rights and peace. Contact the campaign's sponsor at *www.w4peace.org* or 202-588-1471.
- Schedule a prayer service that uses resources prepared by Witness for Peace. The resource "The Economic Way of the Cross" offers a powerful reflection on the sufferings of those who live and work under the crushing weight of global economic injustice. It can be ordered at *www.w4peace.org* or 202-588-1471.

- Raise funds for the Romero Foundation, which is constructing a memorial wall in El Salvador and is also involved in many humanitarian causes in that country. Contact the foundation at *www.romerofoundation.org* or 415-701-1221.
- Watch the movie *Roses in December* (First Run Features, 56 minutes). This award-winning film is both an eloquent memorial to the commitment of Jean Donovan and a powerful indictment of U.S. foreign policy in Central America. Order it from First Run Features at *www.firstrunfeatures.com/vid/roses.html* or 800-229-8575.
- Sponsor a craft fair to help people in impoverished countries like El Salvador. The organization Work of Human Hands helps crafters in such countries to acquire food, education, health care, and housing by developing their skills and establishing self-sustaining businesses. Order a free education kit at *www.catholicrelief.org/what/us_programs/work/index.cfm* or 800-685-7572.
- Encourage the girls to read and discuss *The Weight of All Things,* by Sandra Benitez (New York: Hyperion, 2000). This work of fiction exposes the real tragedy of El Salvador in the 1980s as it tells the tender story of a boy and his grandfather caught between the national military and the procommunist rebels.

Scriptural Connections

- Exod. 4:1–7 (God's sending of Moses)
- 2 Macc. 6:18–31 (The martyrdom of Eleazor)
- Psalm 34 (Deliverance from trouble)
- John 15:18–25 (The world's persecution of disciples)
- Acts 6:8—8:1 (The stoning of Stephen)

Resource Materials

Print

Noone, Judith M. *The Same Fate as the Poor.* Rev. ed. Maryknoll, NY: Orbis Books, 1995.

Zagano, Phyllis. *Ita Ford: Missionary Martyr.* Mahwah, NJ: Paulist Press, 1996.

Internet

www.afsc.org. American Friends Service Committee. Visit the Web site or call 215-241-7000.

www.lawg.org. Latin America Working Group. Visit the Web site or call 202-546-7010.

www.votb.org. Voices on the Border. Visit the Web site or call 202-529-2912.

www.wola.org. Washington Office on Latin America. Visit the Web site or call 202-797-2171.

Background Information:
The Life and Martyrdom of Six Women in El Salvador

A Brief Overview of the Civil War in El Salvador

El Salvador, a Central American country approximately the size of Massachusetts, has struggled since the sixteenth century to maintain peace, justice, and a decent standard of living for all its people. Since the nineteenth century, the politics of El Salvador have been volatile.

During the 1970s, the military of El Salvador were accountable to no one, and the citizens were defenseless against tyranny and oppression. The people of El Salvador suffered increased landlessness, poverty, unemployment, and overpopulation. There was growing unrest as many became more aware of the great social injustices of their peasant economy. Nearly 40 percent of the land was owned by a tiny percentage of the population.

Groups of Christians formed to study, worship, and discuss. These basic communities each elected their own leader. The landowners were alarmed at the sight of uneducated peasants involving themselves with social issues in the name of Christianity. The wealthy conducted virulent press campaigns against the poor, accusing them of practicing Marxism.

In 1972, the military arrested and exiled the elected president and installed their own candidate. The new government unleashed death squads who murdered, tortured, or kidnapped thousands of peasants.

In 1979, civilians overthrew the president and promised reforms. When those reforms did not occur, opposition parties banded together and gained control of areas in the north and east. They blew up bridges, destroyed power lines, and burned coffee plantations in a bid to stifle the country's economy. The military retaliated by destroying villages, causing three hundred thousand citizens to flee the country.

In March 1980, an official death squad assassinated Oscar Romero, the Catholic archbishop of San Salvador, whose weekly sermons broadcast throughout Central America had given hope for change to those who had lived so long without hope.

In November 1989, army officers ordered soldiers to kill six Jesuit priests whose crime had been to open the eyes of their Salvadoran students to the reality of the unjust society in which they lived. The soldiers then killed two witnesses: the Jesuits' housekeeper and her daughter.

Not long after those assassinations, peaceful rallies turned violent as the police opened fire on the crowds. News footage of unarmed demonstrators being gunned down on the steps of the national cathedral turned the eyes of the world to El Salvador.

Eventually, both sides of the conflict approached the United Nations for help in negotiating a settlement. The United Nations sponsored talks, which culminated in the January 1992 signing of peace accords, ending twelve years of civil war.

The Life of Sr. Maura Clarke

Maura Clarke was born 13 January 1931 and lived in Queens, New York. She joined the Maryknoll Sisters in 1950. In 1959, she was sent to a remote city in eastern Nicaragua, where she taught school and did pastoral work.

In 1972, she was working in a parish in the country's capital, Managua, when a devastating earthquake hit the city and killed ten thousand to twenty thousand people. Trapped on an upper floor of the parish house, the Maryknoll sisters climbed down through a window with a rope of sheets and immediately began ministering to the wounded and digging out the dead.

Sister Maura returned to the United States in 1977, to take her turn doing the work of mission and vocation promotion. On 5 August, she answered Archbishop Oscar Romero's appeal for help in El Salvador, where she quickly became immersed in emergency work among victims of the repression. The days were often difficult, and the internal struggle was radically challenging.

In November, Sister Maura, Sr. Ita Ford, and two other Maryknoll sisters traveled to Nicaragua for a regional assembly. There, Sister Maura affirmed her commitment before all the Maryknoll sisters of Central America. She said she would remain in El Salvador, to search out the missing, pray with the families of prisoners, bury the dead, and help the people overcome oppression, poverty, and violence. She told the sisters that the days would be difficult and dangerous, but assured them of her certain confidence in God's loving care of her.

The Life of Jean Donovan

Jean Donovan was born 10 April 1953. She was the younger of two children in an upper-middle-class family in Westport, Connecticut. Her father, Raymond, was an executive engineer, and later chief of design, at the nearby Sikorsky Aircraft Division of United Technologies, a large defense contractor for the United States and a manufacturer of helicopters used in the Vietnam War.

Jean was close to her brother, Michael, who was struck with Hodgkin's disease but made a complete recovery. The experience of the disease and his courageous battle to conquer it left a strong impression on Jean and gave her a deeper sense of the preciousness of life.

Jean received a master's degree in business administration from Case Western Reserve University, then took a job as management consultant for an accounting firm in Cleveland. She was on her way to a successful business career.

But Jean was not content, and began a search for some deeper meaning in life. While volunteering in the Cleveland diocese, she heard about the diocesan mission project in El Salvador. It was what she was looking for.

Jean arrived in El Salvador in July 1979, when the repression was intensifying and the church had become a major target. She became coordinator for the diocesan mission program. In addition to keeping the books, she distributed food and carried out family education programs.

Jean's time in El Salvador challenged her understanding of the meaning of life and faith in a world torn by injustice and violence against the poorest, the most vulnerable.

The Life of Sr. Ita Ford

Ita Ford was born in Brooklyn, New York, on 23 April 1940. After college, in 1961, she joined the Maryknoll Sisters. Health problems forced her to leave the order after three years. This was a difficult personal trial for Sister Ita, as she saw her plans for her life derailed.

After seven years' working as an editor for a publishing company, she reapplied to the Maryknoll Sisters and was accepted. In 1973, she was assigned to Chile, arriving there only a few months before a U.S.-backed military coup overthrew the democratically elected government of Salvador Allende Gossens.

Sister Ita lived in a poor shantytown of Santiago. There, the sisters ministered to the needs of the people during the time of repression, fear, and increased misery for those who were poor. Her years in Chile had a profound impact on Ita.

In 1980, Sister Ita responded to a call for help from El Salvador's archbishop Oscar Romero. In June, she began working with the Emergency Refugee Committee in Chalatenango. Dealing with people who were homeless, persecuted, and victimized by savage repression and war, Sister Ita saw firsthand the Salvadoran reality.

The Life of Sr. Dorothy Kazel

Dorothy Kazel was born 30 June 1939, and joined the Ursuline Sisters, a teaching order in Cleveland, in 1960. Dorothy was engaged to be married when she felt called to the life of a religious sister, and she postponed her marriage to test her calling. She remained with the Ursulines until her death.

Sister Dorothy taught for seven years in Cleveland and later became involved in ecumenical and interracial community programs in the city. In 1974, Sister Dorothy joined the Diocese of Cleveland's mission team in El Salvador. The team consisted of nine members working in three parishes. At first, their main tasks were visiting the homes of parishioners and preparing people for the sacraments.

By the late 1970s, increased repression and political violence were changing the character of the team's work. Sister Dorothy wrote home about the corpses that daily were found along the roadsides. Sister Dorothy's understanding and experience of her own faith were deeply affected by that cruel reality as she shared the suffering of the people and accompanied them in their grief and in their hope.

The Martyrdom of Sister Maura, Jean, Sister Ita, and Sister Dorothy

The destinies of Sr. Maura Clarke, Jean Donovan, Sr. Ita Ford, and Sr. Dorothy Kazel were joined together in just the last months of their lives. On the evening of 2 December 1980, Jean and Sister Dorothy drove to the airport outside San Salvador to pick up Sisters Maura and Ita, who were returning from a Maryknoll regional assembly in Managua. After the four women left the airport, their van was commandeered at a roadblock by members of El Salvador's national guard. They were taken to an isolated location, raped, shot to death, and then buried in a shallow grave along a roadside.

The women are considered martyrs because they did what Jesus of Nazareth did. They loved the poor, and laid down their lives for the poor.

The Life and Martyrdom of Sr. Silvia Maribel Arriola

Silvia Maribel Arriola was born to privileged Salvadorans in 1951. As a child, Silvia was sent to an exclusive Catholic girls' school in San Salvador. Upon graduation, she joined a religious order and was trained as a nurse. Dismantling her identity as a middle-class professional, Sister Silvia took to the base communities of poor people throughout the region. Vowing to work fully and completely with that population, Sister Silvia lived in the slums with four other sisters. She ministered to homeless refugees during the day and attended base community meetings at night.

During this time, popular militant organizations were emerging. This caused tension in the church, and Sister Silvia began to address the church's concern by working with young people in her community. Sister Silvia had a gift for identifying with young people, for being a friend and companion to them.

As the repression expanded, the pastoral team divided into groups to minister in different regions. Sister Silvia was sent to El Amate for a year. A death threat from a paramilitary group forced Sister Silvia to move from village to village out of fear for the families with whom she stayed.

In early January 1981, she was in Santa Ana when it was taken over by government soldiers. Bombs were dropped, cannons were fired, and tanks stormed the clinic. Tracked by radar and pursued by helicopters, Sister Silvia and ninety-one other people ran for three days. On 17 January, they were surrounded and killed. After the slaughter, their bodies were thrown into an open grave.

The Life and Martyrdom of Laura López

Laura López was born and raised in El Salvador. In 1979, Laura went to war-torn Guazapa to join her husband and live as a pastoral worker. Accompanying her were their three small daughters and two sons.

Laura spent a significant amount of time visiting the villages of the area, where she met with the people and conducted various meetings about church issues. She did not fear entering war zones.

Tragedy struck in 1981 when Laura's husband stepped on a land mine and was killed. Her loneliness at times was overwhelming. In addition, Laura's own brothers were members of the government's death squad, and had been ordered to kill her.

In 1985, an air invasion began. Laura recorded and photographed it, and wrote about bombings of innocent people. She sent her observations to the Red Cross, international press agencies, and various Christian churches.

Between December and March, Guazapa was bombed daily. Soon, many people were living under trees or hiding underground, fearing the military. Laura somehow managed to keep the villagers calm and hopeful, while silently she feared that her people would die from hunger. Laura's reflections during weekly liturgies were focused on transformation and resurrection.

On 22 April, the army invaded Guazapa once again. Laura and her family fled to a nearby shelter. When another family arrived at the overcrowded hideout, Laura and her thirteen-year-old daughter left to make space for them. Laura ran into the cane fields, hoping she might find a place to hide until the bombardment ceased. She continued to run even after she was shot, telling her daughter to go forward.

On 27 April, Laura's body was found. As a minister in Guazapa, Laura had refused to abandon her people, and refused to abandon the cause of freedom for the people of El Salvador.

Notes

Use this space to jot ideas, reminders, and additional resources.

A Pledge for Justice and Peace

I pledge to pray about . . .

I pledge to learn more about . . .

I pledge to reach out to . . .

I pledge to live . . .

I pledge to serve . . .

I pledge to give . . .

I pledge to be . . .

Go Out and Be Light

Leader: God of life and light,
Word bringing peace,
Spirit bearing justice,
We give you thanks and praise for
the witness of the dignity of the human person,
sealed by the testimony of these six women:

Sr. Silvia Maribel Arriola, *[Light one pillar candle.]*
Sr. Maura Clarke, *[Light one pillar candle.]*
Jean Donovan, *[Light one pillar candle.]*
Sr. Ita Ford, *[Light one pillar candle.]*
Sr. Dorothy Kazel, *[Light one pillar candle.]*
Laura López. *[Light one pillar candle.]*

And for the countless women martyrs whose names we do not know.

Bless those who create and sustain a culture of life and love. May the candles we light glow bright with
hospitality and hope,
respect and love,
peace and justice.

Loving God, as we raise our voices to you this day in prayer, we are mindful of our sisters and brothers of El Salvador. These are a people who have suffered too long the effects of injustice, repression, civil war, and poverty. So we ask you this day to be strength and courage for the Salvadoran people as we remember this day all people who are
killed in wars.
tortured in jails.
disappearing in the night.
starved for food.
subjected to oppression.
driven from their homes.
unlawfully imprisoned.
denied religious liberty.
excluded from economic opportunity.
marginalized by poverty.
targeted by racial and cultural prejudices.
silenced by violence and injustice.

Knowing that our God walks with us in the darkness, we now come humbly before God to ask for guidance and peace.

Reader 1:   When nations rise against nations,
when killing ends creation.

When dreams are stolen from our hearts,
when fear drives us apart.

All: Grant us peace, Lord. . . .
Grant us your peace.

Reader 2:   When nightmares become reality,
when children turn to brutality.

When silence brings us to tears,
when we can't let go of fears.

All: Grant us peace, Lord. . . .
Grant us your peace.

Reader 3:   When we search and cannot find
answers to stay our minds.

When we cannot find our way,
when we don't have words to say.

When the darkness comes,
scatter our darkness to light!

All: Grant us peace, Lord. . . .
Grant us your peace.

("Grant Us Peace, Lord," as quoted from the album *Fresh as the Morning*,
by Tony Alonso [Chicago: GIA Publications, 2001]. Copyright © 2001
by GIA Publications. Text copyright © 1996 by Hope Publishing Co.,
Chicago, IL. All rights reserved. Used with permission.)

Leader: A prophet is a voice that illuminates the darkness of sin and points the way toward overcoming that darkness. We are called to be light. We do not pass our light to one another as mere ritual or inspiration, something to make us feel good and to look beautiful. We take this light as a commitment to be prophets in our world, to follow the way pointed out to us by Silvia, Maura, Jean, Ita, Dorothy, and Laura.

[Everyone comes to the prayer table, one by one, takes a candle from the basket, lights the candle, and returns with the candle to their place.]

Leader: May your word burn like the word of the prophets. May your defense of the poor and suffering, the victims of injustice and oppression, be a transforming power for our world. May your voice, your feet, your hands, become those of Jesus Christ, building up the Reign of God in our human history. We ask for these blessings, calling on all the martyred victims of injustice and oppression, through God's Son, Jesus Christ, redeemer and savior. Amen.

Carrie Mach

Overview

The previous chapters of this manual present ordinary women who did extraordinary things. Each chapter offers glimpses into the lives of women who embraced their path as the center of meaning for them. Each of those women ventured into unfamiliar places where they never thought they would go, where things were sometimes messy, where they did not know what to expect. Each woman's story highlights moments when life suddenly became bigger, when the woman saw more clearly.

This final chapter offers the girls an opportunity to see how their own actions, wisdom, and beauty make them just as extraordinary as the women they have been studying. The chapter begins with the story of Carrie Mach, a young woman who, in the face of adversity, sought deeper meaning and enjoyment from life.

When Carrie was diagnosed with cancer at the age of nine, she was sad, angry, and scared. When she stopped spending her time wishing away the disease and started using her energy to help others, she experienced a fulfillment she had never known before. Carrie's story is a witness of what is possible for all people when they hear and listen to the voice within.

Thematic Activities

Extraordinary if . . . (40–50 minutes)

Preparation
○ Write the following phrase on newsprint: "You are extraordinary if . . ." Post the newsprint where all can see it.
○ Prepare to give the girls the background information on Carrie Mach from the end of this chapter.

1. Invite the girls to reflect on the women introduced in the previous chapters, and ask them to consider the following questions:

- ◉ What are some common characteristics and qualities possessed by those women?
- ◉ Would you consider those women extraordinary? If so, why?

Invite the girls to share aloud their responses to the questions, and record their responses on the board or on newsprint.

2. Continuing to focus on the women from the previous chapters, ask the girls to call out endings to the sentence-starter you posted earlier. You may need to offer suggestions such as these to get them started:

- ◉ You are extraordinary if, like Saint Jane Frances de Chantal, you can forgive those who have hurt you most.
- ◉ You are extraordinary if, like Sr. Helen Prejean, you can speak out about the sanctity of life.

3. Introduce Carrie Mach by making the following points in your own words:

- ◉ Like the women whose stories we have heard, we have the capacity to live an extraordinary life. Many young women in our communities, parishes, and schools also live ordinary lives in extraordinary ways. It is likely that someone close to you would say that you too are an extraordinary person.
- ◉ We take the time to recognize the way in which all girls can aspire to inspire others. We begin with the story of one such young person.

Provide a brief description of the life of Carrie Mach, being sure to include the following information:

- ◉ Every day, Carrie embraced what the world had to offer. Somehow, she found the energy to move forward, to learn as much as she possibly could.
- ◉ Carrie's favorite quote was, "Don't let what you can't do interfere with what you can" (John Wooden, former UCLA basketball coach). On 29 September 2000, about ten weeks before she died, she wrote in her journal about the things that she could no longer do, but also about things that were important to her like "reading great books, talking to amazing friends, learning how I have made a difference in others' lives. It simply amazes me how such small actions both on my behalf and others, have the ability to change and improve."
- ◉ Carrie's message and example are not unlike those of the women from previous chapters. Those women did not ask why their life unfolded as it did; rather, they asked how. Each woman fully embraced life as she knew it. No matter our age or circumstances, we are all called to do the same.
- ◉ Carrie probably would not have described herself as inspirational, phenomenal, holy, or extraordinary, yet she was all those things. How often do we think that we do not have such qualities? Yet, we are called to celebrate who we are and what we have to give.

4. Divide the girls into groups of four or five. Give each girl one index card for every other person in her group (e.g., if there are four people in the group, each girl will get three cards).

Tell the girls to write the first name of each group member on a separate card, followed by a comma and then the statement "you are extraordinary because . . ." Suggest that they take a few moments to think of a characteristic, quality, accomplishment, or action that they admire for each girl in the group, and to write it on her card. When the girls are done, invite them to take turns acknowledging each member in their group and reading aloud what they wrote about each person.

5. Close the activity with comments like these:
◉ One of Carrie Mach's strongest attributes was her ability to help her friends recognize their unique value and importance. She continually helped those she loved to see how they were special, significant, and appreciated.
◉ We are also called to affirm one another. In doing so, we help one another live more fully and become the extraordinary women God created us to be.

An Extraordinary Wall (30–40 minutes)

Every day, girls in our own communities are making a difference. Their service, personal courage, and creative gifts and talents show us how ordinary human virtues can make us extraordinary. This activity allows the girls to recognize and honor those among them who are making extraordinary choices.

Preparation
○ Cover a wall or a large bulletin board with butcher paper or newsprint.

1. Explain to the girls that they will each have a chance to honor a girl they admire. Allow a few minutes for them to think of someone they want to acknowledge. It could be a close friend, someone they know in the community, or a stranger they have heard or read about.

2. Provide each girl with a sheet of paper. Ask everyone to write a brief biography of the person they chose. You may want to refer to the biography of Carrie Mach as an example of the kinds of things to highlight. Mention that the biography should be no longer than a page.

3. When the girls are done, invite them to come forward individually and tell everyone who they wrote about and why. At the completion of each presentation, direct the girl to write her subject's name on the extraordinary wall, and then tape the biography near it.

4. Consider displaying the extraordinary wall in your parish or school. You might include photos.

Variation. If the group is well established, randomly distribute the members' names, and direct the girls to write biographies about one another.

Developing a Personal Action Plan (20–30 minutes)

Carrie recognized that her life would have much more meaning if she found a way to turn her pain into something useful and meaningful. We also have the opportunity to make our life mean something. This activity allows the girls to explore how they can use their gifts, talents, and experiences for the betterment of others and self.

Preparation

○ Write the following questions on the board:

- Do I work best with people my own age, people younger than me, or people older than me?
- What do I love to do?
- What are some of my areas of interest?
- What specific talents or interests can I share with others?
- What one experience was particularly life changing for me? How can I use it to help others?

1. Instruct the girls to jot their answers to the posted questions. When they are done, ask them to list two or three areas of interest or talents that have surfaced as a result. Note that the questions might have uncovered many areas of interest and talents, and urge the girls to focus on just two or three.

2. Direct the girls to share their lists in pairs or triads, and to brainstorm ways they might put their interests and talents to use. Challenge them to be creative and to consider combining two or more interests or talents into one strategy or approach. Offer an example or two, such as the following ideas:

- ◎ I love to play the piano, and I really appreciate older people. I could play the piano at a retirement home.
- ◎ My grandmother died recently, so I know what it is like to lose someone close to me. Also, I'm really into computer technology. I could create a Web site for teenagers to share memories when they lose someone they love.

3. Encourage the girls to discuss with their partners ways to implement their ideas. At the conclusion of their discussion, they should each have identified a few steps that will help them actually develop a strategy and carry it out. You might pose these questions for them to consider:

- ◎ With whom should I share my idea?
- ◎ Whom should I contact to see if my gifts are needed or would be welcomed?
- ◎ Who do I know that might connect me with an organization or person who needs my particular gifts?
- ◎ What steps do I need to take to make this idea an actuality?

4. If time permits, call the girls to share their ideas with the large group. Invite the girls to offer comments and suggestions to one another.

Prayer Service (10–15 minutes)

This prayer service is based on a speech given by Carrie Mach at Bishop Heelan High School, in Sioux City, Iowa, on Thanksgiving, 1999.

Preparation
○ Create a prayer space by placing a candle and an empty basket on a table.
○ Recruit a volunteer to read an excerpt from Carrie's speech.
○ Make prayer cards from resource 8, "'Life's Greatest Miracle,'" one card for each girl.

1. Gather the girls around the prayer table, give each girl an index card and a pen or pencil, and light the candle on the table. Then begin the service with the following call to prayer:

◉ We pause to offer thanks, to offer our gratefulness for the many blessings we give, and the many blessings we receive. We gather in the name of our Lord, Jesus Christ. We gather with hearts that are full of thanks for a God who helps us appreciate who we are and what we have.

2. Call the volunteer to read the following excerpt from Carrie's speech:

◉ "I encourage each of you to look at your own lives . . . and stop to think about what you are thankful for. Don't go for the easy ones either. Of course you're thankful for your house and food. Stop and really appreciate your parents. . . . Look at the little things, too. When you don't get the A you wanted on a test, be glad you're even getting an education. . . . When you're on your feet all day, be glad you can walk. Even when you just have a bad hair day, thank God for hair. Remember that the little things you take for granted, aren't taken for granted by everyone. Take a new perspective this week. Look at your life from the point of view of someone else. You will be amazed at how many good things you can find."

3. Invite the girls each to write on their index card a word or short phrase about a blessing in their life. This blessing could be a person, an ability, a possession, a trait or characteristic, something profound, or something quite simple—anything that fills their heart with gratitude.

Once they have written their word or phrase, invite them to come forward and read it before placing their card in the basket on the prayer table.

4. Distribute a prayer card to each girl. Then close with the following prayer:

◉ God, divine giver of gifts, we thank you for every day we are given here on earth. We praise you for every breath we take, every obstacle you help us overcome, and every mountain you help us climb. We are thankful for the daily blessings you give us.

Teach us how our greatest obstacles can become your greatest glories. Help us celebrate who we are. Teach us to love ourselves and to accept others. And, God, we pray that you give us the courage and strength to embrace all that life offers us. Amen.

Options and Actions

- Make available a large assortment of crayons or colored pencils. Invite the girls each to create a poster that reads, "If Not Now, Then When?" and hang it where they will see it every day.
- Create a Web page where the girls can log on each day to share moments of gratitude with one another. If Internet access is not available, create a group gratitude journal in which the girls share written reflections with or without sketches, photo collages, and cutout images. Also encourage the girls to use a personal journal to record daily blessings.
- Invite the girls to create a list of the blessings they see in the life of a friend. Note that there is something powerful in hearing about your own blessings from someone else. Invite the girls to present the list to their friend. They might slip it into their friend's locker, send it in the mail or in an e-mail, make an audiotape or videotape of it, or find another creative way to help their friend see the goodness in her life.
- Carrie's favorite quote was "Don't let what you can't do interfere with what you can." Suggest that the girls list all the things they would like to do but cannot for some reason, and a second list of things that are important to them that they can do. Direct them to compare the lists for length. Encourage them to focus their energy on making the things on their "can do" list happen in a way that enriches their world and the world of others.

Scriptural Connections

- Ps. 37:4 (Take delight in God.)
- Josh. 1:9 (Be courageous and do not fear.)
- John 10:10 (Live life to the fullest.)
- Eph. 2:10 (We are created for good works.)
- Phil. 4:13 (I can do all things through Jesus Christ.)

Resource Materials

Print

Fine, Carla. *Strong, Smart, and Bold: Empowering Girls for Life.* New York: Harper-Collins Publishers, Cliff Street Books, 2001.

Gadeberg, Jeanette, and Beth Hatlen. *Brave New Girls: Creative Ideas to Help Girls Be Confident, Healthy, and Happy.* Minneapolis: Fairview Press, 1997.

Internet

www.youthhall.org. International Youth Hall of Fame. This organization helps communities come together to recognize, celebrate, encourage, document, and publicize the positive efforts of their youth who are making a difference at home, in school, and in the community. For more information, visit the Web site or call 206-623-6770.

Background Information:
The Life and Spirituality of Carrie Mach

Inspirational, genuine, spiritual, positive, and *full of life* are just a few words that describe this phenomenal and holy young woman. Carrie Elise Mach was born 2 August 1983. In January 1992, Carrie was diagnosed with a rare form of cancer. In the years that followed, Carrie underwent twelve major surgeries and several rounds of radiation and chemotherapy.

With each obstacle she faced, Carrie learned to embrace and love life more fully. She saw setbacks as an opportunity to deepen her faith and grow closer to God. At the age of twelve, guided by her faith, Carrie suddenly realized that she had a purpose. She found comfort in knowing that, and sought opportunities to reach out—whether by writing letters to others with cancer, writing poetry, or telling her story to people her age. Carrie thought of her situation not as a punishment or burden, but as a continual reminder of how precious each day really is.

Throughout her battle with cancer, Carrie's hometown, Sioux City, Iowa, came to know her through her extensive volunteer work with the Children's Miracle Network and the Make-A-Wish Foundation. Carrie found her true voice in the midst of her illness. She became less afraid to make mistakes and more eager to see what she was made of. She sought challenges, and chose not to settle for mediocrity.

Carrie died 7 December 2000. Even though cancer eventually took Carrie's life, she never allowed it to take her spirit. Her spirit, faith, and determination to make a difference in the world made Carrie a phenomenal and holy young woman who touched lives and changed her world, just by being who God created her to be.

Notes

Use this space to jot ideas, reminders, and additional resources.

"Life's Greatest Miracle"

Life's Greatest Miracle

At times in life, as you are walking, you will feel your feet slip away.
Fear may come to rest beside you, but this feeling will not stay.

God will come when you need Him. This is His promise to you.
And as your feet are slipping, He is figuring out what to do.

It often seems when we need God most, that our faith starts to grow dim.
We are waiting for a miracle, and so forget to trust in Him.

But always look for miracles, no matter how small,
Because the one we never see is the greatest one of all.

(Carrie Mach)

Life's Greatest Miracle

At times in life, as you are walking, you will feel your feet slip away.
Fear may come to rest beside you, but this feeling will not stay.

God will come when you need Him. This is His promise to you.
And as your feet are slipping, He is figuring out what to do.

It often seems when we need God most, that our faith starts to grow dim.
We are waiting for a miracle, and so forget to trust in Him.

But always look for miracles, no matter how small,
Because the one we never see is the greatest one of all.

(Carrie Mach)

Life's Greatest Miracle

At times in life, as you are walking, you will feel your feet slip away.
Fear may come to rest beside you, but this feeling will not stay.

God will come when you need Him. This is His promise to you.
And as your feet are slipping, He is figuring out what to do.

It often seems when we need God most, that our faith starts to grow dim.
We are waiting for a miracle, and so forget to trust in Him.

But always look for miracles, no matter how small,
Because the one we never see is the greatest one of all.

(Carrie Mach)

Strategies for Exploring Phenomenal and Holy Women

Overview

Five additional strategies for helping the girls explore the stories of significant women are described here. Some of the strategies can be done individually; others require small groups of girls. The subjects of the strategies can be any of the women covered in the chapters of this manual, listed in appendix B, or found in the Scriptures, or any other phenomenal women you think of. Most of the strategies should be done over several days or even weeks, because they require the girls to engage in research and creative planning.

Strategies

The Dinner Party

Divide the girls into groups of three and offer the following directions in your own words:

- ❀ Each group is to choose three phenomenal and holy women whose work or experience can be drawn together around one topic for comparison and conversation.
- ❀ Each of you are to research thoroughly one of your group's women and the topic. Your group should plan a dinner party where the three members, each representing one of the women, discuss the topic from their subjects' perspectives. Using your research, you should define your subject's character and try to stay in character throughout the dinner.
- ❀ The dinner can be as elaborate or as simple as you want to make it. Dress in costume and choose culturally appropriate foods.

You may want to provide a set of questions to use as guidelines for the groups' dinner discussions. Many possibilities for topics and groupings exist. Listed below are twelve options:

- *Capital punishment.* Mary, the mother of Jesus; Sr. Helen Prejean; Sojourner Truth
- *Unplanned pregnancies.* Mary, the mother of Jesus; Dorothy Day; Helen Alvare
- *Justice for women.* Mary Magdalene, Hildegard of Bingen, Megan McKenna
- *Political leadership.* Judith, Joan of Arc, Rigoberta Menchú Tum
- *Doing theology.* The woman at the well, Julian of Norwich, Sr. Elizabeth Johnson
- *Church leadership.* Phoebe, Saint Olympias, Bishop Barbara Harris
- *Women in a multicultural world.* Ruth, Sr. Thea Bowman, Silvia Maribel Arriola
- *Creation spirituality.* Eve, Rosemary Haughton, Ada Maria Isasi-Diaz
- *Service to poor people.* Mother Teresa, Saint Louise de Marillac, Saint Katharine Drexel
- *Educational opportunities.* Sor Juana Inés de la Cruz, Mary Ward, Saint Madeleine Sophie Barat
- *Vocation.* Saint Joan of Arc, Jean Donovan, Saint Teresa of Ávila
- *Prayer.* Sr. Joyce Rupp, Saint Jane Frances de Chantal, Saint Thérèse of Lisieux

Variation. Instead of directing the groups each to hold a dinner party, gather the groups and discuss the women, using a talk show format with an emcee. Call the groups to take turns being interviewed, and allow the audience to ask questions and engage in dialogue with the participants.

Church Women Jeopardy

1. Instruct the girls to work in pairs or small groups to create a series of questions like those used in the popular game show *Jeopardy.* You might assign each group a category, such as saints, foundresses, or political activists, and ask each group to develop ten questions about women in its category. Some examples of questions follow:

- With Peter Maurin, she founded the Catholic Worker movement. (*Answer.* Who was Dorothy Day?)
- She founded the Order of Saint Ursula. (*Answer.* Who was Saint Angela Merici?)
- She was a Methodist minister who fought for better working conditions and wages for women in Korea. (*Answer.* Who was Cho Wha Soon?)

You may want to give each girl a list of all the topics or women covered, so that everyone can do some research on their own in preparation for playing the game.

2. Post all the questions in their categories on a wall, and assign a point value to each question. Divide the girls into teams. Announce that the winner of the game will be the team that has the most points. Act as emcee, or appoint someone else to do so, and guide the girls through the game. Consider awarding small prizes or treats to the winning team.

Variation. Address the topics using the format from another popular game show, such as *Who Wants to Be a Millionaire* or *Hollywood Squares.*

Cereal Boxes

Wheaties cereal boxes often feature pictures and biographies of accomplished athletes. Also, special edition cereals have been created with one athlete in mind, such as Flutie Flakes to help Doug Flutie, who was a member of the Buffalo Bills, raise funds for research on autism. The point of this activity is to encourage the girls to create cereal boxes that feature phenomenal women. The project can be done individually or in small groups.

1. Instruct the girls each to choose one woman who they believe should be featured on a cereal box. They are to research that person's life and work, and list all the things that make that person notable. They may use the Internet, books, and whatever other resources are available to them. They should also look for images or pictures of the person, symbols of her work, and so forth.

2. When the girls have completed their research, tell them each to bring in an empty cereal box and decorate it as follows:

- Cover the box with construction paper. On the front, draw a logo for the cereal. The name of the cereal must include the name of the woman you are featuring, such as Blackwell Bits or Catherine Crunch. Also include a photograph or drawing of the person.
- Fill the back of the box with biographical information and highlights of the person's life. You might include pictures or symbols of what this person stood for.
- On one side panel, you might place a bibliography for the person, including Web sites, and books written by and about her.
- On the other side panel, you could present a list of ingredients for your person, such as, "50 percent faith, 20 percent courage, and 30 percent belief in herself."
- You might also include special offers, coupons, and other things that will make the project fun. Be creative.

3. Arrange for everyone to present their cereal boxes to one another. Leave the boxes out for display to the entire school or parish, present them at a parent event, or find other opportunities to share the girls' creativity with the community.

Variation. Have the girls gather information and images to create a set of trading cards, each featuring a phenomenal and holy woman. Model the cards after sports trading cards. Encourage the girls to be creative in the interpretation of items such as team, statistics, and career highlights.

A Chance Encounter

Gather the girls in small groups and direct the groups each to write and present a skit or play in which two to four church women meet by chance and share stories of their life. Historical details are important for the script, but not for the selection of characters.

For example, a medieval woman and an eighteenth-century woman might run into each other waiting for a delayed flight at the airport or in a strength-training class at a local gym. Assign to each group women who have similar interests or are connected by the type of work they do, as in the dinner party idea presented previously.

Variation. Direct the girls each to create their own short video documentary, one-woman play, or magazine feature article about a woman assigned to them.

Pen Pals

Divide the girls into pairs and assign each pair two women from different time periods. The assignments might include women who share similar views and work, such as Saint Clare of Assisi and Caryll Houselander in their work for poor people, or two who hold opposing views, such as Joan of Arc and Dorothy Day in their stands on war and violence.

Direct the partners to write a series of letters to each other over a period of time, as pen pals taking the characters assigned to them. The first letters should be introductory and should include some basic details of their character's life. The other letters can deal with any aspect of their character's life or work, but should include accurate facts and be written from a perspective that is representative of the person.

You may want to specify the number of letters exchanged. You may also want to define the topics for each letter, such as faith, work, and trials and tribulations.

Variation. Assign each girl a contemporary church woman. Explain that the girls are to imagine that they are that woman and that they travel back in time to converse with other church women and write a diary of their experience. You may want to specify that they chronicle only conversations with women whose work or experience is similar to that of their assigned character.

Appendix B

More Phenomenal and Holy Women

Overview

How many other accomplished and extraordinary women are there about whom girls learn little or know nothing? The list of names is almost endless. Girls need to know more about past generations of women so that they may continue to learn from and be inspired by them.

The following list provides a brief overview of other women who have exemplified courage, selflessness, exuberance, and amazing grace. Use the list to expand the girls' exploration of women who have made a difference in the world, possibly with a strategy from appendix A.

Saints, Mystics, and Holy Women

Saint Frances Xavier Cabrini taught and worked in orphanages, taking formal religious vows in 1877. Because no missionary order admitted women at the time, she founded the Missionary Sisters of the Sacred Heart of Jesus.

Saint Catherine of Siena is most remembered for her writings, which eventually led to her being declared a doctor of the church.

Saint Clare of Assisi abandoned all she had to follow God's calling, and became the founder of a religious community of women known as the Poor Clares.

Sor Juana Inés de la Cruz was the first person on the North American continent to argue in writing for women's right to be educated.

Saints Marie d'Oignies, **Hadewijch of Brabant,** and **Mechtilde of Magdeburg** are just a few of the women known as the Beguines. This group of laywomen flourished in the thirteenth century, when the church had defined two legitimate roles for women: cloistered nun and keeper of the home.

Saints Felicity and **Perpetua** were arrested and imprisoned, along with three other Christians, in A.D. 203. Their crime was conversion to Christianity.

Heloise was a highly educated young woman when her legendary correspondence with the philosopher Peter Abelard began. In her letters, she demonstrated that she was well versed in the argument skills of logicians.

At the age of sixteen, **Saint Joan of Arc** heeded God's call and led an army to victory in the Hundred Years' War. She is a national hero of France.

Saint Angela Merici established a community of religious and dedicated young women to respond to the needs of their time. Her community became known as the Order of Saint Ursula.

Saint Elizabeth Ann Seton began a school for Catholic girls. In 1809, she realized a long-cherished dream, taking the vows for a new order that would be known as the Sisters of Charity, the first American order of Catholic nuns.

Saint Edith Stein converted from Judaism to Catholicism and became a devout Carmelite. She died in the gas chamber at Auschwitz in 1942, having been sent to the death camp when she refused to deny her Jewish heritage.

Saint Thérèse of Lisieux lived and taught a spirituality of service, attending to everyone and everything with care and with love.

Mary Ward desired a religious life that would enable her to work outside the walls of a convent. She was a firm believer in education for women, and she made that one of the values of the Loretto Sisters, the religious order she founded.

Other Holy Church Women

Antoinette Brown Blackwell worked throughout her life to validate the public role of women, by challenging traditional barriers that restricted them. She was the first woman minister of a recognized denomination (Congregational), ordained in 1853.

Joan D. Chittister is a Benedictine sister recognized for her work for justice, peace, and equality for women in the church and in society.

Mary Barrett Dyer defied the Puritan church authorities in colonial Boston, to gain religious freedom for Quakers and others. Her martyr's death by hanging helped establish ideas that led to the right to worship freely in the colonies.

Edwina Gately established Genesis House, an urban haven where prostitutes can find safety and calm away from the streets.

Caryll Houselander was an English laywoman who lived through the ravages of World War II. She was the founder of Loaves and Fishes, an organization dedicated to serving the needs of poor people.

Pauli Murray distinguished herself as a lawyer, professor, ordained minister, writer, poet, feminist, and activist who stalwartly confronted racist and sexist acts, throughout the United States.

Elaine Roulet spends her energy and creativity helping the children of women in prison. A sister of Saint Joseph, she has been a family liaison with the Bedford Hills Correction Center, in Bedford Hills, New York, since 1970.

Mother Teresa, the founder of the Missionaries of Charity, fought for the dignity of destitute and dying people in Calcutta. She was known throughout the world for her charity toward poor people and her firm and passionate pro-life stance.

Other Phenomenal Women

Maya Angelou is an internationally respected poet, writer, and educator.

Aung San Suu Kyi is an opposition leader and human rights advocate in Myanmar. In 1991, she won the Nobel Peace Prize for insisting on nonviolence in her country's struggle for democracy.

Cho Wha Soon became a Methodist minister in Korea, where Confucianism and shamanism dictate ethics and cultural norms. She fought for better working conditions and wages for women.

Marian Wright Edelman is a civil rights activist and the founder of the Children's Defense Fund, a strong advocacy group for children.

Dolores Huerta is a respected leader of the labor movement. With Cesar Chavez, she founded the United Farm Workers.

In 1837, **Mary Lyon** founded Mount Holyoke Female Seminary, the first model for institutions of higher education for women in the United States.

Rigoberta Menchú Tum won the Nobel Peace Prize in 1992 for her efforts for peace between Guatemala's majority Indian tribes and minority Spanish-speaking rulers.

Rosa Parks became known as the mother of the U.S. civil rights movement when, in 1955, she refused to give up her seat on a public bus to a white man in Montgomery, Alabama.

Esther Peterson was a catalyst for change in the labor, women's, and consumer movements and the driving force behind the creation of the first Presidential Commission on Women.

Sojourner Truth traveled the United States for over forty years to fight for human rights. She often testified to the demeaning nature of slavery and the redeeming power of faith.

Acknowledgments *(continued from copyright page)*

The scriptural quotations contained herein are from the New Revised Standard Version of the Bible. Copyright © 1989 by the Division of Christian Education of the National Council of the Churches of Christ in the United States of America. All rights reserved.

The first, second, fourth, and fifth guidelines listed on page 14 are paraphrased from *Beyond Nice: The Spiritual Wisdom of Adolescent Girls,* by Patricia H. Davis (Minneapolis: Fortress Press, 2001), pages 119, 120, 121, and 121, respectively. Copyright © 2001 by Augsburg Fortress.

Julian of Norwich's words on pages 20, 21, 22, 24, 25, 25, and 25 are quoted from her *Showings,* translated by Edmund Colledge, OSA, and James Walsh, SJ (New York: Paulist Press, 1978), pages 181, 183, 229, 279, 183, 229, and 342–343, respectively. Copyright © 1978 by the Missionary Society of Saint Paul the Apostle in the State of New York. Used with permission of Paulist Press.

The background information on pages 23–25 is quoted, adapted, and paraphrased from *Praying with Julian of Norwich,* by Gloria Durka (Winona, MN: Saint Mary's Press, 1989), pages 15–23. Copyright © 1989 by Saint Mary's Press. All rights reserved.

The leader comments in step 1 on page 28 are paraphrased from, and the background information on pages 31–32 is quoted, adapted, and paraphrased from, *Praying with Hildegard of Bingen,* by Gloria Durka (Winona, MN: Saint Mary's Press, 1991), pages 91 and 16–27. Copyright © 1991 by Saint Mary's Press. All rights reserved.

The prayer-poem in the first step 3 on page 29 is quoted from Saint Hildegard of Bingen's *Symphonia: A Critical Edition of the "Symphonia armonie celestium revelationum"* ("Symphony of the harmony of celestial revelations"), second edition, translated by Barbara Newman (Ithaca, NY: Cornell University Press, 1998), page 143. Copyright © 1988, 1998 by Cornell University. Used with permission of the publisher, Cornell University Press.

The extract on handout 6 is excerpted from "Litany of Kateri Tekakwitha," by Doris Staton, originally appearing in *Lily,* winter 1987, as quoted at *www.kateritekakwitha.org/kateri/litany.htm,* accessed 26 September 2001.

The background information on pages 70 is based on *Praying with Teresa of Ávila,* by Rosemary Broughton (Winona, MN: Saint Mary's Press, 1990), pages 14–26. Copyright © 1990 by Saint Mary's Press. All rights reserved.

The extract in step 1 on page 76 and the quote in the background information on page 80 are from *Sister Thea Bowman, Shooting Star: Selected Writings and Speeches,* edited by Celestine Cepress, FSPA (La Crosse, WI: Franciscan Sisters of Perpetual Adoration, 1999), pages 76–77 and 117. Copyright © 1999 by Franciscan Sisters of Perpetual Adoration.

The extract in step 2 on page 77 is quoted and adapted from "Prayer Service Honoring Sr. Thea Bowman," by Joseph A. Brown, SJ, in the packet *Celebrating Women Witnesses,* which can be obtained by calling 216-228-0869.

The extract on resource 2 is reprinted from *Sister Thea: Songs of My People, a Compilation of Favorite Spirituals,* by Thea Bowman, FSPA (Boston: St. Paul Books and Media, 1989), page 3. Copyright © 1988 by Daughters of Saint Paul. As quoted in *Sister Thea Bowman, Shooting Star,* edited by Celestine Cepress, pages 43–44. Used with permission of Pauline Books and Media, 50 Saint Paul's Avenue, Boston, MA 02130. All rights reserved.

The words of the United States Conference of Catholic Bishops (USCCB) on page 85 are from the bishops' 1999 statement "A Good Friday Appeal to End the Death Penalty," as quoted at *www.nccbuscc.org/sdwp/national/criminal/appeal.htm,* accessed 10 July 2001. Copyright © 2001 by the USCCB.

The excerpts on resource 3 are quoted from Sr. Helen Prejean's address at the Annual Public Gathering of the American Friends Service Committee on 6 November 1999, as quoted at *www.afsc.org/crimjust/apgprejn.htm,* accessed 9 July 2001. Copyright © American Friends Service Committee. Used with permission.

The reader's words on resource 4 are adapted from a speech given by Helen Prejean, CSJ, at an interreligious service to protest the death penalty, in Albany, New York, on 24 January 1995, as quoted at *www.bway.net/~halsall/radcath/prejean1.html,* accessed 9 July 2001. Copyright © American Friends Service Committee.

The extract on page 92 is adapted from "The Catholic Worker Movement Described in 120 Words," at *www.catholicworker.org/aimsandmeanstext.cfm? Number=6,* accessed 16 July 2001.

The activity "The Magnificent Seven: Catholic Social Teaching," on pages 96–97 is adapted from "The Magnificent Seven: Seven Major Lessons of Catholic Social Teaching," in *Justice and Service Ideas for Ministry with Young Teens,* by Joseph Grant, in the HELP series (Winona, MN: Saint Mary's Press, 2000), pages 91–93. Copyright © 2000 by Saint Mary's Press. All rights reserved.

The words of Dorothy Day in step 1 on page 97, in the third option and action on page 98, and in readings 1, 2, 3, 4, 5, 6, and 10 on resource 7, are quoted from *The Long Loneliness: The Autobiography of Dorothy Day* (New York: Harper and Brothers, Publishers, 1952), pages 283, 285, 285, 132–133, 171, 203, 204, 252, and 286, respectively. Copyright © 1952 by Harper and Row, Publishers. Copyright © renewed 1980 by Tamar Teresa Hennessey. Reprinted by permission of HarperCollins Publishers.

The prayer "Prayer for the Canonization of Servant of God Dorothy Day," on resource 5, is from Claretian Publications, 205 West Monroe Street, Chicago, IL 60606, 312-236-7782, ext. 474, *editors@uscatholic.org,* as quoted at *www.catholicworker. org/dorothyday/index.cfm,* assessed 16 July 2001. Used with permission.

DATE DUE